Freedom of Religion

American Issues in Perspective:
A Documentary Approach

Stanley N. Worton *Series Editor*

Freedom of Religion

Stanley N. Worton

Professor of History
Jersey City State College

HAYDEN BOOK COMPANY, INC.
Rochelle Park, New Jersey

Acknowledgments:

The author expresses his appreciation to Kenneth Worton and David Worton for stimulating his concern for individual liberty. He also wishes to thank the staff of the Forrest A. Irwin Library of Jersey City State College, in particular Mrs. Ruth Arnold, for its generous assistance, and Deena Worton for her encouragement and proof reading.

The author would like to thank the proprietor for permission to quote from the copyrighted work, as follows:
The Clinton Rossiter piece is reprinted from *Seedtime of the Republic,* copyright, 1953, by Clinton Rossiter. Reprinted by permission of Harcourt Brace Jovanovich, Inc.

323
.40973
A512
v. 2

Library of Congress Cataloging in Publication Data

Worton, Stanley N.   comp.
   Freedom of religion.

   (American issues in perspective, a documentary approach)
   Includes bibliographies.
   SUMMARY: Considers important historical documents leading to the establishment of the Bill of Rights and major recent events refining its interpretation, particularly in regards to religious freedom.
   1. Religious liberty — United States — Juvenile literature. [1. Religious liberty. 2. United States — Constitutional law] I. Title.
BR516.W67   323.44'2   74-32381
ISBN 0-8104-6010-6

1	2	3	4	5	6	7	8	9	PRINTING
75	76	77	78	79	80	81	82	83	YEAR

Design: A. Victor Schwarz
Editorial: S. W. Cook
Production: C. McDonald
Consultant: Dr. Abraham Resnick

Introduction

*So, then, to every man his chance—to every man, regardless of his
birth, his shining golden opportunity—to every man the right to live,
to work, to be himself, and to become whatever thing his manhood
and his vision can combine to make—this, seeker, is the promise of
America. I do not believe . . . that the ideas represented by "freedom of thought," "freedom of speech," "freedom of press," and
"free assembly" are just rhetorical myths. I believe rather that they
are among the most valuable realities that men have gained, and that
if they are destroyed men will again fight to have them.*
—Thomas Wolfe

Of Primary Importance

"Congress shall make no law respecting an establishment of religion, or
prohibiting the free exercise thereof; or abridging the freedom of speech or
of the press, or of the right of the people peaceably to assemble, and to petition the government for a redress of grievances"—a sentence of 46 words,
slightly complex in structure, but otherwise seemingly clear in meaning.

It is neither by accident nor by chance that Article I of the Amendments to the Constitution of the United States, the first ten of which com-
prise the Bill of Rights, is first. It heads all the others because the Founding
Fathers recognized that its elements constitute primary liberty: those rights
most essential to individual self-development and the maintenance of a free
society. Nor is it by chance that the various freedoms listed in the First
Amendment are combined in one article. The concern for religion and for
secular thought, expression, and action is an acknowledgment that the human mind is not separated into rigid divisions but instead allows the free
flow of ideas from one area to another. The reasons for opposition to government interference with religious expression are essentially the same as
those for government interference with political expression.

A day does not pass that newspapers and magazines, radio and televi-
sion newscasts, or political speeches do not contain some reference to an issue involving church-state relations, freedom of expression, or the right of
association and participation. In most instances, the items represent poten-
tial threats, if not actual encroachments, upon individual freedoms. Some
maintain that these are insignificant and do not constitute any erosion of civil liberties. Others say they represent a minor diminution, unavoidable when
individual rights are balanced against the internal and external security

needs of a nation in an insecure world. Still others hold that traditional freedoms have become obsolete in an age of insecurity, big government, electronic surveillance, and computer technology, and that we are experiencing a period of repression that could end all First Amendment freedoms. Still others claim that people are less willing than in the past to be told what to do and to leave decisions and their implementation to public officials; people are more assertive, more insistent upon direct participation, and more inclined not to overlook violations of liberty of those outside the established order.

On the other hand, there are those who are totally unaware of any encroachment on freedom and could not care less about civil liberties: A number of years ago during the so-called McCarthy era an enterprising newspaper reporter circulated a petition and solicited signatures in a park on the Fourth of July. The petition contained portions of the Declaration of Independence and the Bill of Rights. Of the more than 100 people approached, only one was willing to sign. Most of those who refused expressed a fear of the consequences if they signed; a number identified the petition as communistic material. A few years later, a group of state civil service employees were unwilling on Bill of Rights Day to have a copy of that document, identified as such, posted on their bulletin board on the grounds that it was a controversial subject. They withdrew their objections only after the governor of the state certified in writing that it was noncontroversial.

Twenty years later, several recent polls show that attitudes have changed but little. One survey revealed the following:

1. 76 percent of those interviewed believe that extremist groups should not be allowed to organize protests against the government even if there is no clear danger of violence.
2. 54 percent feel that not everyone should have the right to criticize the government if the criticism is damaging to national interests.
3. 55 percent think that the mass media should not have the right to report a story if the government feels that it is harmful to the national interest.

In another poll, a majority of Americans were found to support the FBI in bugging and tapping telephones, investigating political protest groups, infiltrating militant protest groups, and keeping dossiers on individuals regardless of whether they were suspected of illegal actions.

Perhaps it is too early to determine with any certainty which view of the state of our civil liberties is correct. Perhaps it will take another three, five, or ten years to see what is "blowin' in the wind." Perhaps you will be the person who will help determine the answers. If this is so, then you unquestionably need to know certain things.

The picture of First Amendment freedoms is a complex one. Its history is long and checkered. It is underlaid with the theory and philosophy of self-development and self-government. It reflects irreconcilable values and is clouded by controversy and conflict. But it is of primary importance.

Because of this, three books in the series *American Issues in Perspective: A Documentary Approach* are devoted to the subject, this volume and *Freedom of Assembly and Petition* and *Freedom of Speech and Press*. In addition, a full examination of the evolution of civil liberties—drawing on the classical philosophers, the Old and New Testaments, the English heritage, and the American experience—is presented in *Freedom of Assembly and Petition,* in the chapter entitled "The Roots of Liberty."

The Libertarian Approach

Before examining the historic development of First Amendment freedoms, a framework of principles and beliefs must be established upon which a clear understanding of the meaning of liberty can be built. The framework here is that of the civil libertarian. Although the reader must think for himself or herself and may very well have different values and draw different conclusions from examining the textual material, interpreting the selections, and responding to the chapter questions, the author hopes that civil libertarian attitudes will prevail.

Liberty, not security, is the goal of society. Much too often, however, even in supposedly democratic countries, it can be violated by governmental as well as nongovernmental forces. Usually, the former are more flagrant and sensational—for example, censorship or police interference with demonstrations. Officials frequently are tempted to suppress dissenters and critics rather than have to vie with them for public support. However, unofficial, nongovernmental violations are more insidious and widespread and, therefore, more effective. They are perpetrated by social pressures stemming from community tradition, custom, or public opinion, which are often intolerant of independent and creative minds. It takes a high degree of civilized restraint for the general citizenry to allow the free expression of opinions that appear hateful and fraught with danger. All past experience shows that the level of liberty in a society becomes set at that provided for the least popular minority.

Without independence of thought and freedom of expression, an official standard of what is right or wrong can come into existence with everyone's loyalty determined by the extent to which he conforms to that standard. Whether orthodoxy results from official or unofficial restraint, the assumption is that all truths are known and that anything that departs from them is heresy or disloyalty. The effect is to destroy freedom of inquiry, constructive criticism, and originality. Without these, new truths cannot be discovered and old ways of doing things cannot be rectified. When a society denounces its dissenters and critics, it cuts itself off from criticism and greatly increases the likelihood of error. One has only to recall the treatment of the abolitionists before the Civil War or the repressions in the McCarthy era to appreciate the effect.

The traditional justification given for suspending or eliminating civil liberties at any given moment in history—from Socrates' time to the present —is that a crisis threatens the safety, if not the very existence, of society. Ironically, democratic freedoms are more vital during crisis. In such times, the welfare of society depends most upon alert, well-informed citizens participating in resolving the crisis. Even if the suspension of specific liberties could be justified by an emergency, any temporary advantages gained would be outweighed by the dangerous precedent established in short-circuiting the democratic process. Liberty, not security, is the goal of government.

It is true that liberties are not absolute, that they may not do harm to society or to its individual members, and that society determines their limits. But drawing the line between the extent and the limit of freedom is one of the most critical tasks of a free society. Frequently, the resolution involves conflicting claims, such as freedom versus security, or the right of privacy versus the freedom of the press, or the right of artistic expression versus the protection of public morals. Such conflicts make the question of liberties vital and fascinating, for both the expert and the student. However, these seeming conflicts are not necessarily conflicting. The civil libertarian sees no real conflict between freedom and security. A society has a basic interest in the rights and well-being of its members; an individual has a vested interest in his society's welfare and stability. In the long run, only a country that encourages free inquiry can solve its problems and preserve its security.

The First Amendment is predicated on the principle that it is not government's business what anyone believes. "The law inspects our actions, our thoughts are left to God." What makes George Orwell's *1984* so frightening to contemplate is the possibility that somewhere, sometime, a person's innermost thoughts could become knowable to a Big Brother. For once minds are enchained, people are reduced to the most total slavery. In a free society, freedom of thought must be absolute. What one believes spiritually or temporally is completely individual. Each seeks truth for himself or herself.

S.W.

Contents

1. In the Name of Religion

*The welfare of the single human soul is the ultimate test of the
vitality of the First Amendment.*

—*William O. Douglas*

Underlying Principles

Religious liberty is enumerated first in the Bill of Rights not by accident but by intent, since it is primary and fundamental. Freedom of conscience was the first, the oldest, and the most strongly desired freedom
throughout history. Most groups had little concern about other freedoms
and were quite willing to sacrifice those in the secular realm in order to protect those in the religious. Leo Pfeffer, an expert on religious freedom,
finds it highly significant that the last substantive article of the original Constitution (Article VII is procedural) ends with a prohibition on any religious tests for office, and the first article of the Bill of
Rights begins with a prohibition against establishment of a national church.
He concludes: "The significance of this ending and beginning is more than
symbolic; it indicates unmistakably that in the minds of the fathers of our
Constitution, independence of religion and government was the alpha and
omega of democracy and freedom."°

Religious liberty is the largest religious freedom for each individual
that can be had without limiting the freedom of others. Since the thoughts of
one cannot interfere with the freedom of thought of any other, there can and
must be complete, limitless liberty of religious thought. However, what one
thinks is rarely ever original, but is generally derived from ideas communi-
cated to him (the thoughts of others); therefore, liberty of religious thought
must embrace liberty of religious communication. Religious acts must also
be free since they are the outward signs of religious thoughts deriving their
meaning from them. If religious acts are not free, religious thoughts cannot
be free. However, they are subject to the same limitation applicable to all
other acts, that they do not impair the equal liberty of all.

Since the purpose of life is the development of character (personality),
which can be developed only where there is freedom of choice, the ability to
follow God's will (religion) is central to existence, and religious liberty is

---

° Leo Pfeffer, *Church, State, and Freedom.* Boston: Beacon Press, 1967, p. 127.

fundamental to all aspects of human liberty and must be equal to all. Religious liberty is not impaired by the influence of other religious thoughts, if it is provided by inspiration, teaching, and example. Rather than restricting the scope of one's will, it expands it by increasing the storehouse of knowledge and concepts. However, where force, conformity, or censorship of religious ideas exists, religious liberty is violated and the purpose of life is repudiated.

Religious liberty exists when the following conditions are met: A church must have a voluntary membership and creed and the right to organize as it wishes, but it cannot use any form of compulsion on members or non-members. The state must require no religious conditions for the full exercise of citizenship, grant no special privileges for adherents of a particular religion, and not interfere for religious reasons with the actions of individuals. Groups should be permitted to practice their codes of moral behavior as long as they do not prevent other groups from freely practicing their own, and government has a responsibility to ensure this.

Religious liberty can exist only when church and state are separated. Separation of church and state involves the use of the power of the state to maintain freedom of religion for all and a prohibition on its power to require any form of religious experience. Separation exists when the state does not use punishment or taxes to obtain conformity of religious practice. The separation of church and state—religious liberty—as it has operated in the United States has been almost unique.

Religious liberty serves to distinguish between man's will to power, which requires limitation, and man's will to perfection, on which no limitation is legitimate. This grew out of a new, radical insight born of the American experience, that it is not government's affair what anyone believes, including what he believes about God. It is the affair of each individual and his God. Religion is thought, feeling, attitude, and faith, and what one believes, no matter how he practices that belief, is so truly individual that government can play no role in it. An establishment of one religion would be a disestablishment of all other religions. Not only can no orthodoxy be required but no heterodoxy can be denied. This is the essence of "free exercise." It means much more than mere toleration, which implies that someone is in possession of "truth" but those who follow "error" will be indulged. The First Amendment was an admission that not only was the colonial experience with toleration a failure, but that it did not serve as a viable philosophy. Those responsible for it recognized that man is not God and that intellectual modesty is more realistic than human omniscience.

The Iron Hand of Orthodoxy

Throughout most of history control of religion was deemed a proper function of government, and the mark of loyalty and conformity to the will of the state was the acceptance of the official religion. Some exceptions to this pattern occurred. In classic Greece and the Roman Republic, religion was an individual matter; although public worship was a state function, individuals could believe as they chose. Even at the beginning of the Christian era Emperor Tiberius announced: "If the gods are insulted, let them see to it themselves." Persecution of early Christians resulted primarily from their public refusals to give even surface recognition to Roman practices, which the state considered a threat to its stability. During the Middle Ages, the Christian Church evolved essentially into an all-powerful, authoritarian institution which commanded the complete allegiance of all its adherents, from kings to peasants, on secular as well as spiritual matters. Punishments for noncomformity did not await the hereafter, and few were willing to incur them. This unity between church and state was antithetical to democracy. As long as the state served as an instrument of the church and individuals were compelled to follow creed, liberty of opinion was impossible. Those outside the church were devoid of all civil rights.

Nevertheless, there were occasional expressions of religious freedom. The church itself provided for the exchange of ideas in periodic international councils; some Christians emphasized direct spiritual experience over dogma; and several "heretical" movements, such as the Waldensians, Hussites, and Lollards, based upon freedom of conscience and individual salvation, broke completely with the church. As feudalism declined and the nation state and the growth in power of kings developed, conflict between church and state became increasingly frequent. The Reformation in the 16th century not only split Christianity into its two principal branches, Catholicism and Protestantism, but split Protestantism as well. The conservative Protestants, such as Lutherans, Calvinists, and Anglicans, maintained close church-state ties, whereas the radical dissenting denominations, such as the Baptists, Quakers, and Unitarians, emphasized liberty.

Religious conflict intensified with the Reformation. A long time passed before the views of a believer in religious toleration, the Swiss Sebastien Castellion, expressed in 1554, gained acceptance: "The time has come to put an end once and for all to this folly that it is necessary to torture and kill men merely because they have other opinions than the powers that be. . . . Killing a man is not upholding a religious principle—it is killing a man."

A summary view of this period found:

> The centuries immediately before and contemporaneous with the colonization of America had been filled with turmoil, civil strife, and persecution, generated in large part by established sects determined to maintain their absolute political and religious supremacy. With the power of government supporting them, at various times and places, Catholics had persecuted Protestants, Protestants had persecuted Catholics, Protestant sects had persecuted other Protestant sects, Catholics of one shade of belief had persecuted Catholics of another shade of belief, and all of these had from time

to time persecuted Jews. In efforts to force loyalty to whatever religious group happened to be on top and in league with the government of a particular time and place, men and women had been fined, cast in jail, cruelly tortured, and killed. Among the offenses for which these punishments had been inflicted were such things as speaking disrespectfully of the views of ministers of government-established churches, non-attendance at those churches, expressions of nonbelief in their doctrines, and failure to pay taxes and tithes to support them.°

In England, a change of monarch meant a different object of persecution. Henry VIII, who instituted the English Reformation, cracked down on any who opposed him, Protestant or Catholic. His successor invoked a law earlier adopted by Catholics to burn heretics as a means of persecuting them. Mary Tudor, a Catholic, used the same statute to execute the Anglican archbishop. Under Elizabeth, Unitarians were burned and other dissenting Protestants persecuted. This situation continued during the 17th century both in England and colonial America. Minority groups that dissented from the established Anglican Church were persecuted in the mother country. In turn, a sect such as the Puritans, who fled to the colonies to avoid repression, zealously persecuted all dissenters from their religion. No group, however, was treated with as much harshness as were the Catholics. The religion was outlawed in England. The Mass could not be practiced even in private, priests were banned from the country under penalty of death, and members of the faith were prohibited from voting or holding public office. As late as 1673, a Test Act was passed by Parliament which was designed to exclude from office all non-Anglicans. In 1689, however, the Toleration Act gave dissenting Protestant sects the right to hold public services and no longer required them to take part in the Anglican worship.

This change of sentiment found its best expression in John Locke's *A Letter Concerning Toleration.* It defined a church as a "voluntary society of men, joining themselves together of their own accord in order to engage in the public worship of God." In a section of the essay, Locke emphasized the principle of separation by stating:

> *First,* Because the care of souls is not committed to the civil magistrate, any more than to other men. It is not committed unto him, I say, by God; because it appears not that God has ever given any such authority to one man over another, as to compel any one to his religion. . . . *In the second place,* The care of souls cannot belong to the civil magistrate because his power consists only in outward force, but true and saving religion consists in the inward persuasion of the mind.

However, the status of Catholics was not significantly altered then. With the advent of the 18th century, there was a rapid secularization of life

---

° *Everson v. Board of Education,* 1947.

and the growth of a live-and-let-live attitude, so that overt persecution of dissent all but disappeared. But not until 1829 were the remaining official restrictions against Catholics finally abolished by Parliament, which removed a ban on Catholics being elected to the House of Commons.

Questions

1. Compare religious freedom in the United States with the situation in any other nation with which you are familiar.
2. Why is religious toleration an inadequate substitute for religious freedom?
3. Why did man's view of life and the afterlife during the Middle Ages and after the Reformation promote religious bigotry and conformity?
4. How did religious conflict in England during the 17th century affect the development of the American colonies?
5. How did each of the European powers other than England, which colonized in what is now the United States, affect religious development in this country?

Suggested Readings

Principles of religious liberty are analyzed in:

Bates, M. Searle. *Religious Liberty: An Inquiry*. New York: International Missionary Council, 1945.

Beth, Loren. *American Theory of Church and State*. Gainesville, Fla.: University of Florida Press, 1958.

Nichols, Roy. *Religion and American Democracy*. Baton Rouge: Louisiana State University Press, 1959.

Pfeffer, Leo. *Creeds in Competition*. New York: Harper & Brothers, 1958.

Snow, Charles. *Religious Liberty in America*. Washington: Review and Herald Publishing Association, 1914.

Early conflicts between orthodoxy and freedom are presented in:

Ehler, Sidney, and Morall, John. *Church and State through the Centuries*. Westminster, Md.: The Newman Press, 1954.

Locke, John. *A Letter Concerning Toleration*. London: J. Johnson, 1800.

Whipple, Leon. *Our Ancient Liberties*. New York: H. W. Wilson Co., 1927.

2. The Care of Souls

If the bell of intolerance tolls for one, it tolls for all.
—*Henry Seidel Canby*

At first the situation in the American colonies was much the same as in England. In New England, the Puritans exacted strict orthodoxy and conformity; in most of the remaining colonies the Church of England, or Anglican Church, was established but not quite so zealously. However, religious uniformity was restricted by geography and was of shorter duration. Almost from the start, dissent and heterodoxy made themselves felt and religious freedom came much faster than it did in the mother country. In addition, as minority religions struggled against established churches to gain recognition and eventual equality, they played an important role in the development of democracy. As the conflict between contending religions became more frequent and disruptive, the concept of the multi-group society gradually developed, one in which religious differences, and differences of belief in general, could exist side by side. This development became the basis of modern democratic doctrine, for it meant that the totality of cultural expression upon which personality is based was no longer subject to the purview of the state. The idea of freedom of conscience spread from those who had religious concerns to those, such as scientists, writers, lawyers, reformers, who had secular concerns.

The Puritan Mind

Probably no single group had more effect on colonial developments than did the Puritans. From their original establishment of Massachusetts Bay, their dominance spread to all of what is New England and their influence was felt in the other colonial sections as well. In England, they had constituted the major dissenting force from the established Anglican Church. Rather than break with it, the Puritans tried to reform or purify it from within, hence their name. They advocated eliminating the system of bishops, the *Book of Common Prayer,* and the elaborate ceremonials, which they felt were all too close to Roman Catholicism. As they gained in numbers and strength in England, they turned to political action and then military force in the Civil War of the 1640s. Those Puritans who despaired of reforming the Anglican Church or wished to avoid the turmoil and persecution of the times became part of the "Great Migration" to America begun in 1629.

Although the Puritans were dissenters who came to the New World to worship as they saw fit without interference and to establish their government on the basis of a Bible commonwealth, they were far from willing to extend freedom, either religious or political, to others. Their leaders, coming as they did primarily from the middle class in England, were now part of the upper class in the colonies. The clergy and the public officials of Puritan New England regarded themselves as stewards of God with whom all authority rested. They had no doubt that they were fitted to rule and that the masses of people were their subjects.

John Cotton was a religious leader of Puritan Massachusetts. Arriving in 1633, he became teacher of the Boston church and before long, because of his scholarship and forceful personality, the dominant voice among the orthodox clergy. He also exercised a strong influence on the government of the Bay Colony, becoming an advisor to Governor John Winthrop. Cotton served as the chief antagonist to Roger Williams in a prolonged theological controversy, which will be dealt with subsequently. The selection that follows is a letter written in 1636 in response to an inquiry made by Lord Say and Seal, one of the few English nobles who was a Puritan. Lord Say and Seal was interested in migrating to the colony, but expressed some reservations about whether the government was democratic and whether his prerogatives would be respected. How does Cotton perceive the relationship between the civil government (commonwealth) and the church? What is his opinion of democracy? In what ways does he reassure Say and Seal? How are Cotton's views on government affected by his religious ideas?

Letter to Lord Say and Seal
John Cotton

It is very suitable to God's all-sufficient wisdom, and to the fullness and perfection of Holy Scriptures, not only to prescribe perfect rules for the right ordering of a private man's soul to everlasting blessedness with himself, but also for the right ordering of a mans family, yea, of the commonwealth too, so far as both of them are subordinate to spiritual ends, and yet avoid both the church's usurpation upon civil jurisdictions, and the commonwealth's invasion upon ecclesiastical administrations, in conformity to the civil state. God's institutions (such as the government of church and of commonwealth be) may be close and compact, and co-ordinate one to another, and yet not confounded. God hath so framed the state of church government and ordinances, that they may be compatible to any commonwealth, though never so much disordered in his frame. But yet when a commonwealth hath liberty to mold his own frame I conceive the scripture hath given full direction for the right ordering of the same, and that, in such sort as may best maintain the strength of the church. Mr. Hooker doth often quote a saying out of Mr. Cartwright (though I have not read it in him) that no man fashioneth his house to his hangings, but his hangings to his house. It is better that the commonwealth be fashioned to the setting forth of God's house, which is his church, than to accommodate the church frame to the civil state. Democracy, I do not conceive that ever God did ordain as a fit government either for church or commonwealth. If the people be governors, who shall be governed? As for monarchy, and aristocracy, they are both of them clearly approved, and directed in scripture, yet so as referreth the sovereign to himself, and setteth up Theocracy in both, as the best form of government in the commonwealth, as well as in the church. . . .

When your Lordship doubteth, that this course will draw all things under the determination of the church, (seeing the church is to determine who shall be members, and none but a member may have to do in the government of a commonwealth) be pleased (I pray you) to conceive, that magistrates are neither chosen to office in the church, nor do govern by directions from the church, but by civil laws, and those enacted in general courts, and executed in courts of justice, by the governors and assistants. In all which, the church (as the church) hath nothing to do: only, it prepareth fit instruments both to rule, and to choose rulers, which is no ambition in the church, nor dishonor to the commonwealth; the apostle, on the contrary, thought it a great dishonor and reproach to the church of Christ, if it were not able to yield able judges to hear and determine all causes amongst their brethren, I Cor. vi. 1 to 5, which place alone seemeth to me fully to decide this question; for it plainly holdeth forth this argument: It is a shame to the church to want able judges of civil matters and an audacious act in any church member voluntarily to go for judgment, other where than before the saints then it will be no arrogance nor folly in church members, nor prejudice to the commonwealth, if voluntarily they never choose any civil judges, but from amongst the saints, such as church members are called to be. But the former is clear: and how then can the latter be avoided. If this therefore be (as your Lordship rightly conceiveth) one of the main objections if not the only one which hindereth this commonwealth from the entertainment of the propositions of those worthy gentlemen, we intreat them, in the name of the Lord Jesus, to consider, in meekness of wisdom, it is not any conceit or will of ours, but the holy counsel and will of the Lord Jesus (whom they seek to serve as well as we) that overruleth us in this case: and we trust will overrule them also, that the Lord only may be exalted amongst all his servants. What pity and grief were it, that the observance of the will of Christ should hinder good things from us! . . .

Nor need we fear, that this course will, in time, cast the commonwealth into distractions, and popular confusions. For (under correction) these three things do not undermine, but do mutually and strongly maintain one another (even those three which we principally aim at) authority in magistrates, liberty in people, purity in the church. Purity, preserved in the church, will preserve well ordered liberty in the people, and both of them establish well balanced authority in the magistrates. God is the author of all these three, and neither is himself the God of confusion, nor are his ways the ways of confusion, but of peace. . . .

*   *   *

The government of Massachusetts may best be categorized as a theocratic oligarchy. A fundamental regulation required that, "No man shall be admitted to the freedom of this body politic, but such as are members of some of the churches within the limits of the same." In other words, in order to be a freeman or citizen entitled to sit on the General Court, the law-making body of the colony, one had to be, in addition to an adult male property holder, a member of the church; and to be a member of the church one had to be approved by the clergy. When the government was first established, only twelve of the initial population of 2,000 were freemen. Hence, the colony was ruled by an oligarchy, and since these civil leaders were handpicked by the ministry, the government was theocratic.

Although the Puritans remained nominally Anglican, their religious beliefs were closely akin to Calvinism. They were not followers of the Reformationist leader John Calvin, but arrived at their doctrines on their own through their interpretation of the Bible. Placing great stress on original sin, they believed in the total depravity of man. Only by God's grace could anyone be saved. No one could know whether he was of the "elect" or the damned; nor did anyone have any control over his fate. Thus, the Puritans believed in predestination by which God determined in advance whether or not an individual would be saved, and nothing that he did during his lifetime could make any difference. However, Puritanism differed from Calvinism in one respect; it was not as dogmatic. Since the Puritans had arrived at their beliefs by means of an intellectual process, they allowed an element of reason to exist in their theology. They felt that a person's actions throughout his lifetime might reflect the degree of inner grace given him by God; leading a good life could not save you, but because you were predestined to be saved you were able to lead a good life. Since damnation in Hell was eternal, the Puritans had a strong compulsion to conform to a strict moral code of behavior, in the hope that this might indicate that they were among the elect.

As the Puritans began to prosper, their Calvinistic beliefs about salvation and damnation were extended to include the material world. Financial success came to be regarded as another outward visible sign of inner spiritual grace. Those who attained it were clearly of the elect.

The autocratic religious and political views that dominated Puritan thought, first in Massachusetts and then throughout New England, did not go unchallenged. Since all aspects of Puritan life were dominated by religious beliefs, not surprisingly, those who tried to promote democratic liberty did so in religious terms. Religious and political dissent were indivisible. Attacks on civil authority were viewed as an attack on God's law, and attacks on the established church were an attack on established civil authority. The dissenters, branded as heretics, came from the ranks of English Independents, who preached the principles of congregationalism—the democratic organization of church government—and the right of the individual to determine his own beliefs. One such group, the Pilgrims or Separatists, had broken with the Church of England before they came to America as an expression of their firmly held belief that religion was private and should be free of government interference. They formed into autonomous congregations that would be more responsive to their faith and ideals. The Mayflower Compact adopted on November 11, 1620, was an extension of the church compact idea to the realm of civil government. Unfortunately, their colony of Plymouth was evenutally absorbed into the more populous and powerful Massachusetts Bay Colony which surrounded it.

Of all the dissenters in America, the most important, because his beliefs were the most far reaching and his actions the most effective, was Roger Williams. Shortly after his arrival in Massachusetts in 1631, he became identified with Separatism and began to preach doctrines that antagonized both church leaders and civil magistrates. He insisted that the charter granted to the Massachusetts Bay Company was fraudulent, because the land given by the king belonged to the Indians, since they had not sold or ceded it by treaty. He also opposed the colony's laws requiring oaths of allegiance of all inhabitants, church attendance, and the payment of a tax to support the church. He asserted that these regulations constituted interference by the state in religious matters. These challenges were more than the authorities would tolerate. Williams was summoned before the General Court. When he refused to correct his errors, he was placed on trial in October, 1635, found guilty of heresy, and sentenced to be banished by deportation back to England. (If he had not been a minister, he probably would have been put to death). He escaped into the wilderness, taking up with the Narragansett Indians, whom he had earlier befriended. He was subsequently joined by sympathizers and other dissenters like Ann Hutchinson to form Rhode Island.

Williams set down his ideas on religious and political liberty in several tracts written in a running dispute with John Cotton. The most important of these was *The Bloudy Tenent of Persecution,* which was published in 1644. What follows is the Preface. What does the title mean? Why does he believe that it is wrong for the state to interfere in religious matters? Why is he opposed to uniformity of belief? What does he assert in the last clause?

The Bloudy Tenent of Persecution
Roger Williams

First, That the blood of so many hundred thousand souls of Protestants and Papists, spilt in the Wars of present and former Ages, for their respective Consciences, is not required nor accepted by Jesus Christ the Prince of Peace.

Secondly, Pregnant Scriptures and Arguments are throughout the Work proposed against the Doctrine of persecution for the cause of Conscience.

Thirdly, Satisfactory Answers are given to Scriptures, and objections produced by Mr. Calvin, Beza, Mr. Cotton, and the Ministers of the New English Churches and others former and later, tending to prove the Doctrine of persecution for cause of Conscience.

Fourthly, The Doctrine of persecution for cause of Conscience, is proved guilty of all the blood of the Souls crying for vengeance under the Altar.

Fifthly, All Civil States with their Officers of justice in their respective constitutions and administrations are proved essentially Civil, and therefore not Judges, Governors or Defenders of the Spiritual or Christian state and Worship.

Sixthly, It is the will and command of God, that (since the coming of his Son the Lord Jesus) a permission of the most Paganish, Jewish, Turkish, or Antichristian consciences and worships, be granted to all men in all Nations and Countries: and they are only to be fought against with that Sword which is only (in Soul matters) able to conquer, to wit, the Sword of God's Spirit, the Word of God.

Seventhly, The state of the Land of Israel, the Kings and people thereof in Peace & War, is proved figurative and ceremonial, and no pattern nor precedent for any Kingdom or civil state in the world to follow.

Eighthly, God requireth not an uniformity of religion to be enacted and inforced in any civil state; which enforced uniformity (sooner or later) is the greatest occasion of civil War, ravishing of conscience, persecution of Christ Jesus in his servants, and of the hypocrisy and destruction of millions of souls.

Ninthly, in holding an enforced uniformity of Religion in a civil state, we must necessarily disclaim our desires and hopes of the Jews' conversion to Christ.

Tenthly, an enforced uniformity of Religion throughout a Nation or civil state, confounds the Civil and Religious, denies the principles of Christianity and civility, and that Jesus Christ is come in the Flesh.

Eleventhly, The permission of other consciences and worships then a state professeth, only can (according to God) procure a firm and lasting peace, (good assurance being taken according to the wisdom of the civil state for uniformity of civil obedience from all sorts.)

Twelfthly, lastly, true civility and Christianity may both flourish in a state or Kingdom, notwithstanding the permission of divers and contrary consciences, either of Jew or Gentile.

*   *   *

Postscript

Cotton's response to *The Bloudy Tenent* presents a clear picture of the orthodox Puritan mind at work. He agreed that to force men against their conscience into certain beliefs is indeed persecution. But no man's conscience can compel him to reject the truth, and, therefore, to force the truth upon him is not a violation of conscience. Furthermore, offenders should be subject to temporal punishments, since these punishments might arouse them from their sin and ignorance and bring about their repentance. In short, these doctrines justified the Puritans' use of force: they were in the right, whereas other religions were in the wrong. This completely denied what Williams called the "two tables." This doctrine held that the state could deal only with man's relations to his fellow man; it had no right to interfere in man's relations to God, which belonged to the church. But beyond this, *The Bloudy Tenent* called for complete religious liberty, and its underlying philosophy recognized the critical linkage between the right of individual conscience and separation of church and state.

Roger Williams was perhaps the greatest American civil libertarian of the 17th century because he carried his beliefs in religious freedom over into the political realm and he practiced what he preached. The colony of Rhode Island and Providence Plantations which he founded and headed (against his will) was the most democratic commonwealth in colonial times. Church and state were separate, there were no religious qualifications for voting, and under Williams' governorship, limited government, local autonomy, and individualism flourished. As might be expected, the colony became a refuge for persecuted religious minorities. The Rhode Island Code of 1647 stipulated that "all men may walk as their consciences persuade them, every one in the name of God." Williams welcomed Quakers, who were being persecuted as "cursed heretics" and hanged in Massachusetts, even though he disagreed with their beliefs and tried to persuade them to change. The colony became a refuge for Baptists, who organized a fellowship in 1639, the first in the colonies. The first synagogue in America was built at Newport. But because of the religious and ethnic diversity, the colony lacked unity and singleness of purpose and, therefore, remained small and weak. It had no backing from a wealthy proprietor or a group of merchants; in fact, its neighbors tried to subvert its existence.

In 1633, the colony finally obtained an official charter from the Crown. It provided that "no person . . . shall be in any wise molested, punished, disquieted or called in question, for any differences in opinion in matters of religion, and do not actually disturb the civil peace of our said colony." However, following Williams' death, there was a significant retrenchment of liberties. Citizenship and the right to hold office were limited to Protestants; however, this regulation was not consistently enforced, and some Catholics and Jews did obtain citizenship. More important, they were not subject to overt persecution.

Dissenting Minorities

Outside of New England, diversity was greater and dissent more successful. This was especially true of the colonies founded by proprietors. Obliged to recruit settlers, they attracted groups that were ethnically and religiously more varied and tended, therefore, to be more tolerant. Maryland was a good example of this, particularly since it involved the most persecuted religious minority at the time—Catholics.

George Calvert, the first Lord Baltimore and a convert to Catholicism, founded the colony of Maryland in 1632 both as a haven for his fellow religionists and as a business venture. Almost from the outset, more Protestants than Catholics were attracted to the colony. Recognizing this trend and wishing to avoid future sectarian conflict, as well as trying to remain in the good graces of the English government, Cecilius, the second Lord Baltimore, instructed the General Assembly to adopt a toleration act. Reflecting in part proprietary principles of religious liberalism and in part proprietary self-interest and expediency, *An Act Concerning Religion* was passed in 1649. It was the first statute in America providing for religious toleration. It meant that official recognition was given to Protestants and Catholics living side by side at peace with one another—for the times, a revolutionary conception. What religious belief did one have to hold in order to live securely in the colony? What types of actions were subject to punishment? What forms did the punishments take? Why is this considered an act of toleration rather than of liberty?

An Act Concerning Religion, 1649

Forasmuch as in a well governed and Christian Common Wealth matters concerning Religion and the honor of God ought in the first place to be taken, into serious consideration and endeavored to be settled. Be it therefore ordered and enacted by the Right Honorable Cecilius Lord Baron of

Baltimore absolute Lord and Proprietary of this Province with the advise and consent of this General Assembly. That whatsoever person or persons within this Province and the Islands thereunto belonging shall from henceforth blaspheme God, that is Curse him, or deny our Saviour Jesus Christ to be the son of God, or shall deny the holy Trinity the Father son and holy Ghost, or the Godhead of any of the said Three persons of the Trinity or the Unity of the Godhead, or shall use or utter any reproachful Speeches, words or language concerning the said Holy Trinity, or any of the said three persons thereof, shall be punished with death and confiscation or forfeiture of all his or her lands and goods to the Lord Proprietary and his heirs, And be it also Enacted by the Authority and with the advise and assent aforesaid. That whatsoever person or persons shall from henceforth use or utter any reproachful words or Speeches concerning the blessed Virgin Mary the Mother of our Saviour or the holy Apostles or Evangelists or any of them shall in such case for the first offence forfeit to the said Lord Proprietary and his heirs Lords and Proprietaries of this Province the sum of Five pound Sterling or the value thereof to be Levied on the goods and chattels of every such person so offending, but in case such Offender or Offenders, shall not then have goods and chattels sufficient for the satisfying of such forfeiture, or that the same be not otherwise speedily satisfied that then such Offender or Offenders shall be publicly whipt and be imprisoned during the pleasure of the Lord Proprietary or the Lieutenant or chief Governor of this Province for the time being. And that every such Offender or Offenders for every second offence shall forfeit ten pound sterling or the value thereof to be levied as aforesaid. . . . And that every person or persons before mentioned offending herein the third time, shall for such third Offence forfeit all his lands and Goods and be for ever banished and expelled out of this Province. And be it also further Enacted by the same authority advise and assent that whatsoever person or persons shall from henceforth upon any occasion of Offence or otherwise in a reproachful manner or Way declare call or denominate any person or persons whatsoever inhabiting residing trafficking trading or commercing within this Province or within any the Ports, Harbors, Creeks or Havens to the same belonging an heretic, Scismatic, Idolator, puritan, Independent, Presbyterian popish priest, Jesuit, Jesuited papist, Lutheran, Calvinist, Anabaptist, Brownist, Antinomian, Barrowist, Roundhead, Seperatist, or any other name or term in a reproachful manner relating to matter of Religion shall for every such Offence forfeit and lose the sum of ten shillings sterling or the value thereof to be levied on the goods and chattels of every such Offender and Offenders, the one half thereof to be forfeited and paid unto the person and persons of whom such reproachful words are or shall be spoken or uttered, and the other half thereof to the Lord Proprietary and his heirs Lords and Proprietaries of this Province, But if such person or persons who shall at any time utter or speak any such reproachful words or Language shall not have Goods or Chattels sufficient and overt within this Province to be taken to satisfy the penalty aforesaid or that the same be not otherwise speedily satisfied, that then the person or persons so offending shall be publicly whipt, and shall suffer imprisonment without bail or mainprise until he, she or they respectively shall satisfy the party so offended or grieved by such reproachful Language by asking him or her respectively forgiveness publicly for such his Offence before the Magistrate or chief Officer or Officers of the Town or place where such Offence shall be given. And be it further likewise Enacted by the Authority and consent aforesaid That every person and persons within this Province that shall at any time hereafter profane the Sabbath or Lord's day called Sunday by frequent swearing, drunkenness or by any uncivil or disorderly recreation, or by working on that day when absolute necessity doth not require it shall for every such first offence forfeit 2*s*, 6*d* sterling or the value thereof, and for the second offence 5*s* sterling or the value thereof, and for the third offence and so for every time he shall offend in like manner afterwards 10*s* sterling or the value thereof. And in case such offender and offenders shall not have sufficient goods or chattels within this Province to satisfy any of the said Penalties respectively hereby imposed for profaning the Sabbath or Lord's day called Sunday as aforesaid, That in Every such case the party so offending shall for the first and second offence in that kind be imprisoned till he or she shall publicly in open Court before the chief Commander Judge or Magistrate, of that County Town or precinct where such offence shall be committed acknowledge the Scandal and offence he hath in that respect given against God and the good and civil Government of this Province. And for the third offence and for every time after shall also be publicly whipt. And whereas the enforcing of the conscience in matters of Religion hath frequently fallen out to be of dangerous Consequence in those commonwealths where it hath been practised, And for the more quiet and peaceable government of this Province, and the better to preserve mutual Love and amity amongst the Inhabitants thereof. Be it Therefore also by the Lord Proprietary with the advise and consent of this Assembly Ordained & enacted (except as in this present Act is before Declared and set forth) that no person or persons whatsoever within this Province, or the Islands, Ports, Harbors, Creeks, or havens thereunto belonging professing to believe in Jesus Christ, shall from henceforth be any ways troubled, Molested or discountenanced for or in respect of his or her religion nor in the free exercise thereof within this Province or the Islands thereunto belonging nor any way compelled to the belief or exercise of any other Religion against his or her consent, so as they be not unfaithful to the Lord Proprietary, or molest or conspire against the civil Government established or to be established in this Province under him or his heirs. And that all & every person and persons that shall presume Contrary to this Act and the true intent and meaning thereof directly or indirectly either in person or estate willfully to wrong disturb trouble or molest any person whatsoever within this Province professing to believe in Jesus Christ for or in respect of his or her religion or the free exercise thereof within this Province other than is provided for in this Act that such person or persons so offending, shall be compelled to pay treble damages to the party so wronged or molested, and for every such offence shall also forfeit 20s sterling in money or the value thereof, half thereof for the use of the Lord Proprietary, and his heirs Lords and Proprietaries of this Province, and the other half for the use of the party so wronged or molested as aforesaid. . . . And be it further also Enacted by the authority and consent aforesaid That the Sheriff or other Officer or Officers from time to time to be appointed & authorized for that purpose, of the County Town or precinct where every particular offence in this present Act contained shall happen at any time to be committed and whereupon there is hereby a Forfeiture Fine or penalty imposed shall from time to time distrain and seize the goods and estate of every such person so offending as aforesaid against this present Act or any part thereof, and sell the same or any part thereof for the full satisfaction of such forfeiture, Fine, or penalty as aforesaid, Restoring unto the party so offending the Remainder or overplus of the said goods or estate after such satisfaction so made as aforesaid.

*   *   *

Postscript

Measured against current standards, or even those of the Revolutionary period, the act does not seem very liberal, but judged by the degree of toleration elsewhere at that time, it constituted a milestone. Unfortunately, before the century was out, the Baltimores lost political control of Maryland, the Anglican Church was established, additional Catholics were barred from entrance, and those already settled were forbidden to celebrate Mass in public.

More than any other denomination, the Quakers or Society of Friends were involved in the issues of religious diversity and dissent. Founded in England by George Fox, they were the most independent of the sects that broke with the Anglican Church. Believing as they did in the "inner light," which provided intuitive truth and spiritual guidance to each individual, many of them practiced their faith without creed, church, ministry, or service. Instead, they held a "meeting," where one or all could participate as their consciences moved them. Because of these beliefs, the form of worship, and the Friends zealous efforts to convert others, they were severely persecuted at home and in America, where a number fled. The colony that treated them the worst was Massachusetts. Quakers were beaten, tarred-and-feathered, jailed, tortured, or, in a few instances, put to death.

The reception afforded the Quakers in America was not uniform. Some attempted to settle in New Netherland under the Dutch. During the 17th century, Holland was the most tolerant country in Europe. The English Pilgrims, or Separatists, had settled there before founding Plymouth. Likewise, the first Jews to come to America settled in New Amsterdam in 1654, although with some difficulty. Three years later a small number of Quakers attempted to find refuge in Flushing (Vlishing), now Queens, New York City. But Peter Stuyvesant, the tyrannical governor of New Netherland, acted to keep them out. He issued a proclamation making it an offense for any of the townspeople to shelter a Quaker. A strong protest to this eventually led Stuyvestant to back down. The following selection is the brief remonstrance. Why do the people refuse to obey Stuyvesant's order? How do they justify their action through the Bible? How do you feel about their views? In what way is this selection an expression of religious liberty?

The Flushing Remonstrance

Right Honorable

You have been pleased to send up unto us a certain petition or command that we should not receive or entertain any of those people called Quakers because they are supposed to be by some, seducers of the people. For our part we cannot condemn them in this case neither can we stretch out our hands against them, to punish, banish or persecute them, for out of Christ God is a consuming fire, and it is a fearful thing to fall into the hands of the living God.

We desire therefore in this case not to judge least we be judged, neither to condemn least we be condemned, but rather let every man stand and fall to his own Master. We are bound by the Law to do good unto all men, especially to those of the household of faith. And though for the present we seem to be unsensible of the law and the Law giver, yet when death and the Law assault us, if we have our advocate to seek, who shall plead for us in this case of conscience betwixt God and our own souls; the powers of this world can neither attack us, neither excuse us, for if God justify who can condemn and if God condemn there is none can justify.

And for those jealousies and suspicions which some have of them, that they are destructive unto Magistracy and Ministery, that can not be, for the magistrate hath the sword in his hand, and the minister hath the sword in his hand, and witness those two great examples which all magistrates and ministers are to follow, Moses and Christ, whom God raised up maintained and defended against all the enemies both of flesh and spirit; and therefore that which is of God will stand, and that which is of man will come to nothing. And as the Lord hath taught Moses or the civil power to give an outward liberty in the state by the law written in his heart designed for the good of all, and can truly judge who is good, who is evil, who is true and who is false, and can pass definitive sentence of life or death against that man which rises up against the fundamental law of the States General; so he hath made his ministers a savor of life unto life, and a savor of death unto death.

The law of love, peace and liberty in the states extending to Jews, Turks, and Egyptians, as they are considered the sons of Adam, which is the glory of the outward state of Holland, so love, peace and liberty, extending to all in Christ Jesus, condemns hatred, war and bondage. And because our Saviour saith it is impossible but that offenses will come, but woe unto him by whom they cometh, our desire is not to offend one of his little ones, in whatsoever form, name or title he appears in, whether Presbyterian, Independent, Baptist or Quaker, but shall be glad to see anything of God in any of them, desiring to do unto all men as we desire all men should do unto us, which the true law both of Church and State; for our Saviour saith this is the law and the prophets.

Therefore if any of these said persons come in love unto us, we cannot in conscience lay violent hands upon them, but give them free egress and regress unto our Town, and houses, as God shall persuade our consciences. And in this we are true subjects both of Church and State, for we are bound by the law of God and man to do good unto all men and evil to no man. And this is according to the patent and charter of our Town, given unto us in the name of the States General which we are not willing to infringe, and violate, but shall hold to our patent and shall remain, your humble subjects, the inhabitants of Vlishing.

*   *   *

Following the takeover of New Netherland by the British in 1664 and its division into New York and New Jersey, the Quakers found another haven in a section of the latter known as West Jersey. The province came under the ownership in 1676 of several Quaker proprietors, one of them the great democrat William Penn. His document, "Laws, Concessions, and Agreements," gave to the people the most liberal constitution of its time. Included in it was the proviso: "That no man, nor number of men upon earth, hath power or authority to rule over men's consciences in religious matters."

From his experience in West Jersey, Penn developed the idea of establishing a new colony of his own expressly as a place for Quakers who were being persecuted elsewhere. But from the time that Pennsylvania was launched in 1682, it was open to people of all faiths and persisted as the most liberal colony down to the Revolution. The Quakers had a marked effect on the development of religious diversity, and because of their explicit and literal belief in the brotherhood of man, their influence was significant on other matters such as education, pacifism, Indian affairs, and slavery.

By mid-18th century, the Friends were well established in New Jersey and Pennsylvania, free from the persecutions that had earlier beset them. Because of their sense of dedication and hard work, a number had become well off, if not prosperous. One of their number, John Woolman, became concerned about such material success and in the following selection extracted from *A Journal of the Life . . . of John Woolman,* written between 1756 and 1772, expressed the essence of a "Quaker conscience." Born in Mt. Holly, New Jersey, he was at various times a clerk, missionary, teacher, tailor, and merchant. What can you learn from the story concerning a will about how Quakers influence others? How would you describe the various Friends' meetings Woolman attends? Why is he opposed to material success? What does he do about it?

Journal
John Woolman

Scrupling to do writings relative to keeping slaves, has been a means of sundry small trials to me, in which I have so evidently felt my own will set aside, I think it good to mention a few of them. Tradesmen and retailers of goods, who depend on their business for a living, are naturally inclined to keep the good will of their customers; nor is it a pleasant thing for young men to be under any necessity to question the judgment or honesty of elderly men, and more especially of such as have a fair reputation. Deep-rooted customs, though wrong, are not easily altered; but it is the duty of all to be firm in that which they certainly know is right for them. A charitable, benevolent man, well acquainted with a negro, may I believe, under some circumstances, keep him in his family as a servant, on no other motives than the negro's good; but man, as man, knows not what shall be after him, nor hath he any assurance that his children will attain to that perfection in wisdom and goodness, necessary rightly to exercise such power; hence it is clear to me, that I ought not to be the scribe where wills are drawn, in which some children are made absolute masters over others during life.

About this time, an ancient man of good esteem in the neighborhood, came to my house to get his will written. He had young negroes; and I asked him privately how he purposed to dispose of them. He told me; I then said, I cannot write thy will without breaking my own peace; and respectfully gave him my reasons for it. He signified that he had a choice that I should have written it; but as I could not, consistently with my conscience, he did not desire it; and so he got it written by some other person. A few years after, there being great alterations in his family, he came again to get me to write his will. His negroes were yet young; and his son, to whom he intended to give them, was, since he first spoke to me, from a libertine, become a sober young man; and he supposed that I would have been free on that account to write it. We had much friendly talk on the subject, and then deferred it. A few days after he came again, and directed their freedom; and I then wrote his will. . . .

Having found drawings in my mind to visit friends on Long Island, after obtaining a certificate from our monthly meeting, I set off twelfth of fifth month, 1756. When I reached the island, I lodged the first night at the house of my dear friend Richard Hallet. The next day, being the first of the week, I was at the meeting in New Town; in which we experienced the renewed manifestations of the love of Jesus Christ, to the comfort of the honest-hearted. I went that night to Flushing; and the next day, I and my beloved friend Matthew Franklin, crossed the ferry at White Stone; were at three meetings on the main, and then returned to the island; where I spent the remainder of the week in visiting meetings. The Lord I believe hath a people in those parts, who are honestly inclined to serve him; but many, I fear, are too much clogged with the things of this life, and do not come forward bearing the cross in such faithfulness as He calls for.

My mind was deeply engaged in this visit, both in public and private; and, at several places where I was, on observing that they had slaves, I found myself under a necessity, in a friendly way, to labor with them on that subject; expressing as way opened, the inconsistency of that practice with the purity of the Christian religion, and the ill effects of it manifested amongst us.

The latter end of the week their yearly meeting began; at which were our friends John Scarborough, Jane Hoskins, and Susannah Brown, from Pennsylvania. The public meetings were large, and measurably favored with divine goodness. The exercise of my mind, at this meeting, was chiefly on account of those who were considered as the foremost rank in the society; and in a meeting of ministers and elders, way opened for me to express in some measure what lay upon me; and when friends were met for transacting the affairs of the church, having sat a while silent, I felt a weight on my mind, and stood up; and through the gracious regard of our heavenly Father, strength was given fully to clear myself of a burden, which for some days had been increasing upon me.

Through the humbling dispensations of Divine Providence, men are sometimes fitted for his service. The messages of the prophet Jeremiah were so disagreeable to the people, and so adverse to the spirit they lived in, that he became the object of their reproach; and in the weakness of nature, he thought of desisting from his prophetic office; but saith he, "His word was in my heart as a burning fire shut up in my bones; and I was weary with forbearing, and could not stay." I saw at this time, that if I was honest in declaring that which truth opened in me, I could not please all men; and I labored to be content in the way of my duty, however disagreeable to my own inclination. After this I went homeward, taking Woodbridge and Plainfield in my way; in both which meetings, the pure influence of divine love was manifested; in an humbling sense whereof I went home. I had been out about twenty-four days, and rode about three hundred and sixteen miles.

While I was out on this journey, my heart was much affected with a sense of the state of the churches in our southern provinces; and believing the Lord was calling me to some further labor amongst them, I was bowed in reverence before Him, with fervent desires that I might find strength to resign myself to his heavenly will.

Until this year, 1756, I continued to retail goods, besides following my trade as a tailor; about which time I grew uneasy on account of my business growing too cumbersome. I had begun with selling trimmings for garments, and from thence proceeded to sell cloths and linens; and at length, having got a considerable shop of goods, my trade increased every year, and the way to large business appeared open; but I felt a stop in my mind.

Through the mercies of the Almighty, I had, in a good degree, learned to be content with a plain way of living. I had but a small family; and on serious consideration, believed truth did not require me to engage much in cumbering affairs. It had been my general practice to buy and sell things really useful. Things that served chiefly to please the vain mind in people, I was not easy to trade in; seldom did it; and whenever I did, I found it weaken me as a Christian.

The increase of business became my burden; for though my natural inclination was toward merchandise, yet I believed truth required me to live more free from outward cumbers: and there was now a strife in my mind between the two. In this exercise my prayers were put up to the Lord, who graciously heard me, and gave me a heart resigned to his holy will. Then I lessened my outward business; and as I had opportunity, told my customers of my intentions, that they might consider what shop to turn to; and in a while I wholly laid down merchandise, and followed my trade as a tailor by myself, having no apprentice. I also had a nursery of apple-trees; in which I employed some of my time in hoeing, grafting, trimming, and inoculating. In merchandise it is the custom, where I lived, to sell chiefly on credit, and poor people often get in debt; when payment is expected, not having wherewith to pay, their creditors often sue for it at law. Having frequently observed occurrences of this kind, I found it good for me to advise poor people to take such goods as were most useful, and not costly. . . .

Every degree of luxury hath some connection with evil; and if those who profess to be disciples of Christ, and are looked upon as leaders of the people, have that mind in them which was also in Christ, and so stand separate from every wrong way, it is a means of help to the weaker. As I have sometimes been much spent in the heat, and have taken spirits to revive me, I have found by experience, that in such circumstances the mind is not so calm, nor so fitly disposed for divine meditation, as when all such extremes are avoided. I have felt an increasing care to attend to that holy Spirit which sets right bounds to our desires; and leads those who faithfully follow it, to apply all the gifts of Divine Providence to the purposes for which they were intended. Did those who have the care of great estates, attend with single-ness of heart to this heavenly instructor, which so opens and enlarges the mind, as to cause men to love their neighbors as themselves, they would have wisdom given them to manage their concerns, without employing some people in providing the luxuries of life, or others in laboring too hard, but for want of steadily regarding this principle of divine love, a selfish spirit takes place in the minds of people, which is attended with darkness, and manifold confusions in the world.

Though trading in things useful is an honest employ; yet through the great number of superfluities which are bought and sold, and through the corruption of the times, they who apply to merchandise for a living, have great need to be well experienced in that precept which the prophet Jeremiah laid down for his scribe; "seekest thou great things for thyself? seek them not."

*   *   *

These movements of dissent, toleration, and nonconformity did not go unchallenged or unchecked. Religious leaders of more orthodox and tradi-tional churches and their conservative allies in government attempted to hold on to the minds of the people and maintain old-time religion. Certainly no one was more dedicated in this effort than were the Puritans.

During the 1680s, Massachusetts lost its original charter and the new one issued in 1691 converted it into a royal colony. The legal authority of the oligarchy was terminated and the theocratic relationship between the civil rulers and the Puritan clergy was broken. Much to the chagrin of the leader-ship, these circumstances coupled with the disburbances caused by the Glo-rious Revolution created unrest and confusion in the colony. The unrest was followed by one of the most famous episodes of colonial times— the Salem witchcraft trials. It should be noted that belief in witchcraft had persisted in Europe for centuries, and those suspected of consorting with the devil were generally tried and executed. What made Salem unique, at least for America, was that the hysteria that erupted in 1691 and 1692 did not abate until 19 persons had been hung, one had been pressed to death, and 55 others had confessed!

Less dramatic and gory, but longer lasting, was another effort to coun-teract nonconformity and freethinking in religion. This was a revivalist movement that became known as the Great Awakening. Starting at the turn of the 18th century in New Jersey, Pennsylvania, and Massachusetts, it soon spread to every colony. Led by Jonathan Edwards, outstanding theologian and philosopher, and itinerant evangelist George Whitefield, it won new converts and brought tens of thousands back to religion with renewed fer-vor. Traditional forms of worship were abandoned; instead of formal services, preachers resorted to physical exhortation, excessive emotional display, and the public repentance of sinners. These practices caused a sensation among the uneducated masses and popularized the movement.

Questions

1. Show how the Puritans were both a force for intellectual stagnation and a force for intellectual development in America.
2. Second only to Roger Williams as a Puritan dissenter was the heroic Ann Hutchinson. What were the reasons for her split with the church leaders?
3. Compare the treatment of Quakers, Catholics, and Jews during colonial times.
4. Which colonies during the 18th century experienced the widest religious diversity and what were the reasons for this?
5. Although the Puritan clergy did not provoke the witchcraft hysteria, why did they allow it to work its course?
6. What residue of Puritanism can you find in American life today?

Suggested Readings

Puritan thought and practice are dealt with in:

Miller, Perry. *The New England Mind: The Seventeenth Century*. Cambridge: Harvard University Press, 1954.

Morison, Samuel E. *The Intellectual Life of Colonial New Egland*. New York: New York University Press, 1956.

Perry, Ralph. *Puritanism and Democracy*. New York: Vanguard Press, 1944.

Winslow, Ola. *Master Roger Williams, a Biography*. New York: Macmillan, 1957.

The status of minority religions during colonial times is found in:

Blau, Joseph. *Cornerstones of Religious Freedom in America*. New York: Harper & Row, 1949.

Bridenbaugh, Carl. *The Mitre and the Scepter*. New York: Oxford University Press, 1962.

Goodman, Abram. *American Overture: Jewish Rights in Colonial Times*. Philadelphia: Jewish Publications Society of America, 1947.

Marnell, William. *The First Amendment: The History of Religious Freedom in America*. Garden City, N.Y.: Doubleday & Co., 1964.

Mecklin, Joseph. *The Story of American Dissent*. New York: Harcourt, Brace & Co., 1934.

Meyer, Jacob. *Church and State in Massachusetts from 1740 and 1833*.

3. No Right to Intrude

The greatest achievement ever made in the cause of human progress is the total and final separation of church and state. If we had nothing else to boast of, we could lay claim with justice that first among the nations we of this country made it an article of organic law that the relations between man and his Maker were a private concern, into which other men have no right to intrude. To measure the stride thus made for the Emancipation of the race, we have only to look back over the centuries that have gone before us, and recall the dreadful persecutions in the name of religion that have filled the world.

—David Dudley Field

Evolving Religious Freedom

Despite all efforts to hold them in check, the spirit of secularization and of toleration proceeded rapidly in the colonies during the 18th century. The factors contributing to this were a decline in the hatreds engendered by the Reformation and the religious wars that followed it, which created a live-and-let-live attitude both in England and in the colonies; the expansion of settlements westward, which made it difficult to maintain established institutions such as churches and ordained clergy, and which, in turn, gave rise to the camp meeting and self-appointed itinerant preacher; the large number of religious groups that sprang up on American soil, which meant that no single denomination could control the entire social order, thus making persecution of dissent impracticable; and the secularism and humanism that grew out of the American and French revolutions and had a strong effect upon intellectual development.

In addition, another important factor was at work. During the 17th century, when the role of the state had been strong, the associations formed for educational, cultural, philanthropic, business, as well as religious purposes, were looked upon as adjuncts of the state. They were so by custom or were made so by charter. In this capacity they acted under the authority of the government and were rewarded with special privileges. In religion, the majority churches in each of the colonies alone enjoyed this status; minority sects were excluded. By the 18th century, dissenting religious associations were forming without legal recognition. They began to act like corporations or voluntary associations even though they were not entitled to do so. This was caused by the diversity of the population, particularly in the cosmopolitan centers of New York, Philadelphia, and Newport, where a number of different religions flourished side by side. Even though separation of church and state was not to come until after the Revolution, the advantages of union diminished well before. All religious bodies, established or voluntary, were relatively new and poor and had to compete with each other for membership. Those without legal recognition were not prevented from acquiring and holding property. Finally, the congregational form of church organization further weakened the influence of government in religion. Thus, practical circumstances provided a strong reinforcement to the principles of separation of church and state.

The church-state question came to a head when England attempted to tie the religious life in the colonies closer to that of the mother country by setting up an Anglican bishopric in America. Opposition was immediate and vocal from both Anglicans and non-Anglicans. One of the strongest protests came from a Boston minister, Jonathan Mayhew, himself an Anglican. He published his views in 1763 in a pamphlet entitled *Observations on the Charter and the Conduct of the Society for the Propagation of the Gospel in Foreign Parts,* from which the following selection is taken. What does Mayhew find wrong with the Church of England? Why is he against the sending of a bishop to America? What does he mean by his reference to Columbus? Why does he resurrect from English history the attempt by the Crown to impose the Anglican religion on the Scots?

Observations on the Propagation of the Gospel
Jonathan Mayhew

When we consider the real constitution of the church of England; and how alien her mode of worship is from the simplicity of the gospel, and the apostolic times: When we consider her enormous hierarchy, ascending by various gradations from the dirt to the skies: When we consider the visible effects of that church's prevailing among us to the degree that it has: When we reflect on what our Forefathers suffered from the mitered, lordly SUC-CESSORS *of the fishermen of Galilee,* for non-conformity to a non-instituted mode of worship; which occasioned their flight into this western world: When we consider that, to be delivered from their unholy zeal and oppressions, countenanced by scepter'd tyrants, they threw themselves as it were into the arms of Savages and Barbarians: When we reflect, that one principal motive to their exchanging the fair cities, villages, and delightful fields of Britain for the then inhospitable shores and deserts of America, was, that they might here enjoy, unmolested, God's holy word and ordinances, without such heterogenous and spurious mixtures as were offensive to their well-informed consciences: When we consider the narrow, censorious and bitter spirit that prevails in too many of the episcopalians among us; and what might probably be the sad consequence, if this growing party should once get the upper hand here, and a major vote in our houses of *Assembly:* (in which case the church of England might become the established religion here; *tests* be ordained, as in England, to exclude all but conformists from posts of honor and emolument; and all of us be taxed for the support of *bishops* and their *underlings:*) When we consider these things, and too many others to be now mentioned, we cannot well think of that church's gaining ground here to any great degree, and especially of seeing bishops fixed among us, without much reluctance—Will they never let us rest in peace, except *where all the weary are at rest?* Is it not enough, that they persecuted us out of the old world? Will they pursue us into the new to convert us here?—*compassing sea and land to make* US *proselytes,* while they neglect the heathen and heathenish plantations! What other new world remains as a sanctuary for us from their oppressions, in case of need? Where is the COLUMBUS to explore one for, and pilot us to it, before we are consumed by the flames, or deluged in a flood of episcopacy? . . .

One of our Kings, it is well known, excited his Scotch subjects to take up arms against him, in a great measure, if not chiefly, by attempting to force the English liturgy upon them, at the instigation of the furious episcopal zealots of that day; by whom he was wheedled and duped to his destruction. But GOD be praised, we have a KING, whom Heaven long preserve and prosper, too wise, just and good to be put upon any violent measures, to gratify men of such a depraved turn of mind.

*   *   *

Few men better exemplified the secularism, humanism, and rationalism of the 18th century than did Benjamin Franklin. Printer, writer, scientist, inventor, philosopher, and statesman, he best represented the American ideal of the self-educated, self-made man who, from humble beginnings, became materially successful, internationally renowned, and his country's elder statesman. The following selection, taken from his famous *Autobiography* written in the 1770s and 1780s, shows how he developed his freethinking ideas. Why did he turn away from organized religion? Which traditional beliefs did he retain and which did he reject? What is your reaction to his 13 virtues? Bearing in mind what you know of Franklin's life, what do you think of his program of self-improvement?

Autobiography
Benjamin Franklin

I have been religiously educated as a Presbyterian; and tho' some of the dogmas of that persuasion, such as *the eternal decrees of God, election, reprobation, etc.,* appeared to me unintelligible, others doubtful, and I early absented myself from the public assemblies of the sect, Sunday being my studying day, I never was without some religious principles. I never doubted, for instance, the existence of the Deity, that he made the world, and govern'd it by his Providence; that the most acceptable service of God was the doing good to man; that our souls are immortal; and that all crime will be punished, and virtue rewarded, either here or hereafter. These I esteem'd the essentials of every religion; and, being to be found in all the religions we had in our country, I respected them all, tho' with different degrees of respect, as I found them more or less mix'd with other articles, which, without any tendency to inspire, promote, or confirm morality, serv'd principally to divide us, and make us unfriendly to one another. This respect to all, with an opinion that the worst had some good effects, induc'd me to avoid all discourse that might tend to lessen the good opinion another might have of his own religion; and as our province increas'd in people, and new places of worship were continually wanted, and generally erected by voluntary contribution, my mite for such purpose, whatever might be the sect, was never refused.

Tho' I seldom attended any public worship, I had still an opinion of its propriety, and of its utility when rightly conducted, and I regularly paid my annual subscription for the support of the only Presbyterian minister or meeting we had in Philadelphia. He us'd to visit me sometimes as a friend, and admonish me to attend his administrations, and I was now and then prevail'd on to do so, once for five Sundays successively. Had he been in my opinion a good preacher, perhaps I might have continued, notwithstanding the occasion I had for the Sunday's leisure in my course of study; but his discourses were chiefly either polemic arguments, or explications of the peculiar doctrines of our sect, and were all to me very dry, uninteresting, and unedifying, since not a single moral principle was inculcated or enforc'd, their aim seeming to be rather to make us Presbyterians than good citizens.

At length he took for his text that verse of the fourth chapter of Philippians, *"Finally, brethren, whatsoever things are true, honest, just, pure, lovely, or of good report, if there be any virtue, or any praise, think on these things."* And I imagin'd, in a sermon on such a text, we could not miss of having some morality. But he confin'd himself to five points only as meant by the apostle, viz.: 1. Keeping holy the Sabbath day. 2. Being diligent in reading the holy Scriptures. 3. Attending duly the public worship. 4. Partaking of the Sacrament. 5. Paying a due respect to God's ministers. These might be all good things; but, as they were not the kind of good things that I expected from that text, I despaired of ever meeting with them from any other, was disgusted, and attended his preaching no more. I had some years before compos'd a little Liturgy, or form of prayer, for my own private use (viz., in 1728), entitled, *Articles of Belief and Acts of Religion.* I return'd to the use of this, and went no more to the public assemblies. My conduct might be blamable, but I leave it, without attempting further to excuse it; my present purpose being to relate facts, and not to make apologies for them.

It was about this time [ca. 1730] I conceiv'd the bold and arduous project of arriving at moral perfection. I wish'd to live without committing any fault at any time; I would conquer all that either natural inclination, custom, or company might lead me into. As I knew, or thought I knew, what was right and wrong, I did not see why I might not always do the one and avoid the other. But I soon found I had undertaken a task of more difficulty than I had imagined. While my care was employ'd in guarding against one fault, I was often surprised by another; habit took the advantage of inattention; inclination was sometimes too strong for reason. I concluded, at length, that the mere speculative conviction that it was our interest to be completely virtuous, was not sufficient to prevent our slipping; and that the contrary habits must be broken, and good ones acquired and established, before we can have any dependence on a steady, uniform rectitude of conduct. For this purpose I therefore contrived the following method.

In the various enumerations of the moral virtues I had met with in my reading, I found the catalogue more or less numerous, as different writers included more or fewer ideas under the same name. Temperance, for example, was by some confined to eating and drinking, while by others it was extended to mean the moderating every other pleasure, appetite, inclination, or passion, bodily or mental, even to our avarice and ambition. I propos'd to myself, for the sake of clearness, to use rather more names, with fewer ideas annex'd to each, than a few names with more ideas; and I included under thirteen names of virtues all that at that time occurr'd to me as necessary or desirable, and annexed to each a short precept, which fully express'd the extent I gave to its meaning.

The names of virtues, with their precepts, were:

1. *Temperance.* Eat not to dullness; drink not to elevation.
2. *Silence.* Speak not but what may benefit others or yourself; avoid trifling conversation.
3. *Order.* Let all your things have their places; let each part of your business have its time.
4. *Resolution.* Resolve to perform what you ought; perform without fail what you resolve.
5. *Frugality.* Make no expense but to do good to others or yourself; *i.e.,* waste nothing.

6.   *Industry*. Lose no time; be always employ'd in something useful; cut off all unnecessary actions.

7.   *Sincerity*. Use no hurtful deceit; think innocently and justly, and, if you speak, speak accordingly.

8.   *Justice*. Wrong none by doing injuries, or omitting the benefits that are your duty.

9.   *Moderation*. Avoid extremes; forbear resenting injuries so much as you think they deserve.

10.   *Cleanliness*. Tolerate no uncleanliness in body, clothes, or habitation.

11.   *Tranquility*. Be not disturbed at trifles, or at accidents common or unavoidable.

12.   *Chastity*. Rarely use venery but for health or offspring, never to dullness, weakness, or the injury of your own or another's peace or reputation.

13.   *Humility*. Imitate Jesus and Socrates.

My intention being to acquire the *habitude* of all these virtues, I judg'd it would be well not to distract my attention by attempting the whole at once, but to fix it on one of them at a time; and, when I should be master of that, then to proceed to another, and so on, till I should have gone thro' the thirteen; and, as the previous acquisition of some might facilitate the acquisition of certain others, I arrang'd them with that view, as they stand above. Temperance first, as it tends to procure that coolness and clearness of head, which is so necessary where constant vigilance was to be kept up, and guard maintained against the unremitting attraction of ancient habits, and the force of perpetual temptations. This being acquir'd and establish'd, Silence would be more easy; and my desire being to gain knowledge at the same time that I improv'd in virtue, and considering that in conversation it was obtain'd rather by the use of the ears than of the tongue, and therefore wishing to break a habit I was getting into of prattling, punning, and joking, which only made me acceptable to trifling company, I gave *Silence* the second place. This and the next order, I expected would allow me more time for attending to my project and my studies; *Resolution,* once become habitual, would keep me firm in my endeavors to obtain all the subsequent virtues; *Frugality* and Industry freeing me from my remaining debt, and producing affluence and independence, would make more easy the practice of Sincerity and Justice, etc., etc. . . .

*   *   *

The most influential development of the 18th century leading toward rationalism was the philosophy-religion of Deism. A product of the Age of the Enlightenment, it had its origins with Voltaire and other French intellectuals. It spread to England and the New World, where it was embraced by some of the leading figures of American life: Thomas Jefferson, Benjamin Franklin, John Adams, Thomas Paine, and, from time to time, George Washington. The Deists were directly influenced by natural law, reason, and science, especially the new astronomy and geology. They rejected traditional theology, revelation, and ritual and considered the Bible as the work of man, not the word of God. They believed in God as "first cause," the creator of the universe, who once he set it in motion became its "retired architect." The universe was able to govern itself following God's immutable laws, laws that were comparable to the laws of motion that controlled the physical world. Thus, there was no purpose in worshipping God or having organized religious institutions. Because of its mechanistic quality, cold rationalism, and lack of spiritual and emotional warmth, Deism found acceptance only among the intellectual few and was rejected by the mass of people. Nevertheless, its influence was profound. It helped to reduce superstition and dogmatism and promote tolerance and rationalism, and directly affected the American and French revolutions. Any doubts about the first revolution can be allayed by a reading of the Declaration of Independence.

The most potent expression of Deism in America came from the pen of Thomas Paine. The fiery pamphleteer had been a hero of the American Revolution. His *Common Sense* did more than anything else to arouse the patriotic fervor of the colonists and impel them to rebellion. His *Crisis Papers* were given the highest praise by General Washington. Following the war, he went to France to promote revolution there, but was subsequently forced to flee from the Reign of Terror. While in England, he wrote the *Age of Reason,* which was published in 1794 and for which he was excoriated and shunned when he returned to the United States. He died here a broken and penniless man. What follows are extracts from that work. Why did he write it? Fully explain his statement: "My own mind is my own church." Why does he focus his criticism of organized religions on Christianity and why does he accuse it of atheism? How does the Deist show his love of God? If Paine was not an atheist, why was he reviled and accused of being one?

Age of Reason

Thomas Paine

To My Fellow-Citizens of the United States of America

I put the following work under your protection. It contains my opinion upon religion. You will do me the justice to remember that I have always strenuously supported the right of every man to his own opinion, however different that opinion might be to mine. He who denies to another this right makes a slave of himself to his present opinion, because he precludes himself the right of changing it. The most formidable weapon against errors of every kind is reason. I have never used any other, and I trust I never shall.

Your affectionate friend and fellow citizen,

Thomas Paine

It has been my intention for several years past to publish my thoughts upon Religion. I am well aware of the difficulties that attend the subject; and from that consideration had reserved it to a more advanced period of life. I intended it to be the last offering I should make to my fellow-citizens of all nations, and that at a time when the purity of the motive that induced me to it could not admit of a question, even by those who might disapprove the work.

The circumstance that has now taken place in France, of the total abolition of the whole national order of priesthood and of everything appertaining to compulsory systems of religion and compulsory articles of faith, has not only precipitated my intention, but rendered a work of this kind exceedingly necessary; lest, in the general wreck of superstition, of false systems of government, and false theology, we lose sight of morality, of humanity, and of the theology that is true.

As several of my colleagues, and others of my fellow-citizens of France, have given me the example of making their voluntary and individual profession of faith, I also will make mine; and I do this with all that sincerity and frankness with which the mind of man communicates with itself.

I believe in one God, and no more; and I hope for happiness beyond this life.

I believe in the equality of man, and I believe that religious duties consist in doing justice, loving mercy, and endeavoring to make our fellow-creatures happy.

But lest it should be supposed that I believe many other things in addition to these, I shall, in the progress of this work, declare the things I do not believe and my reasons for not believing them.

I do not believe in the creed professed by the Jewish church, by the Roman church, by the Greek church, by the Turkish church, by the Protestant church, nor by any church that I know of. My own mind is my own church.

All national institutions of churches—whether Jewish, Christian, or Turkish—appear to me no other than human inventions set up to terrify and enslave mankind and monopolize power and profit.

I do not mean by this declaration to condemn those who believe otherwise. They have the same right to their belief as I have to mine. But it is necessary to the happiness of man that he be mentally faithful to himself.

Infidelity does not consist in believing or in disbelieving; it consists in professing to believe what he does not believe.

It is impossible to calculate the moral mischief, if I may so express it, that mental lying has produced in society. When a man has so far corrupted and prostituted the chastity of his mind as to subscribe his professional belief to things he does not believe, he has prepared himself for the commission of every other crime. He takes up the trade of priest for the sake of gain, and in order to *qualify* himself for that trade, he begins with a perjury. Can we conceive anything more destructive to morality than this?

Soon after I had published the pamphlet, *Common Sense,* in America, I saw the exceeding probability that a revolution in the system of government would be followed by a revolution in the system of religion. The adulterous connection of church and state, wherever it had taken place, whether Jewish, Christian, or Turkish, had so effectually prohibited, by pains and penalties, every discussion upon established creeds and upon first principles of religion, that until the system of government should be changed those subjects could not be brought fairly and openly before the world; but that whenever this should be done, a revolution in the system of religion would follow. Human inventions and priestcraft would be detected, and man would return to the pure, unmixed, and unadulterated belief of one God, and no more. . . .

As to the Christian system of faith, it appears to me as a species of atheism; a sort of religious denial of God. It professes to believe in a man rather than in God. It is a compound made up chiefly of manism, with but little deism, and is as near to atheism as twilight is to darkness. It introduces between man and his Maker an opaque body, which it calls a Redeemer, as the moon introduces her opaque self between the earth and the sun; and it produces by this means a religious or an irreligious eclipse of light. It has put the whole orb of reason into shade.

The effect of this obscurity has been that of turning everything upside down and representing it in reverse; and among the revolutions it has thus magically produced, it has made a revolution in theology.

That which is now called natural philosophy, embracing the whole circle of science of which astronomy occupies the chief place, is the study of the works of God, and of the power and wisdom of God and his works, and is the true theology.

As to the theology that is now studied in its place, it is the study of human opinions and of human fancies *concerning* God. It is not the study of God himself in the works that he has made, but in the works or writings that man has made; and it is not among the least of the mischiefs that the Christian system has done to the world that it has abandoned the original and beautiful system of theology, like a beautiful innocent, to distress and reproach, to make room for the hag of superstition.

The book of Job and the 19th Psalm, which even the church admits to be more ancient than the chronological order in which they stand in the book called the Bible, are theological orations conformable to the original system of theology. The internal evidence of those orations proves to a demonstration that the study and contemplation of the works of creation, and of the power and wisdom of God revealed and manifested in those works, make a great part of the religious devotion of the times in which they were written; and it was this devotional study and contemplation that led to the discovery of the principles upon which what are now called sciences are established; and it is to the discovery of these principles that almost all the arts that contribute to the convenience of human life owe their existence. Every principal art has some science for its parent, though the person who mechanically performs the work does not always, and but very seldom, perceive the connection.

It is a fraud of the Christian system to call the sciences *human inventions;* it is only the application of them that is human. Every science has for its basis a system of principles as fixed and unalterable as those by which the universe is regulated and governed. Man cannot make principles; he can only discover them.

For example. Every person who looks at an almanac sees an account when an eclipse will take place, and he sees also that it never fails to take place according to the account there given. This shows that man is acquainted with the laws by which the heavenly bodies move. But it would be something worse than ignorance were any church on earth to say that those laws are a human invention.

It would also be ignorance or something worse to say that the scientific principles, by the aid of which man is enabled to calculate and foreknow when an eclipse will take place, are a human invention. Man cannot invent anything that is eternal and immutable, and the scientific principles he employs for this purpose must be, and are, of necessity, as eternal and immutable as the laws by which the heavenly bodies move, or they could not be used as they are to ascertain the time when, and the manner how, an eclipse will take place. . . .

It is from the study of the true theology that all our knowledge of science is derived, and it is from that knowledge that all the arts have originated.

The Almighty lecturer, by displaying the principles of science in the structure of the universe, has invited man to study and to imitation. It is as if he had said to the inhabitants of this globe that we call ours: "I rendered the starry heavens visible, to teach him science and the arts. He can now provide for his own comfort, AND LEARN FROM MY MUNIFICENCE TO BE KIND TO EACH OTHER." . . .

Having now extended the subject to a greater length than I first intended, I shall bring it to a close by abstracting a summary from the whole.

First—That the idea or belief of a word of God existing in print, or in writing, or in speech, is inconsistent in itself for the reasons already assigned. These reasons, among others, are the want of a universal language; the mutability of language; the errors to which translations are subject; the possibility of totally suppressing such a word; the probability of altering it, or of fabricating the whole, and imposing it upon the world.

Secondly—That the creation we behold is the real and ever-existing word of God in which we cannot be deceived. It proclaimeth his power, it demonstrates his wisdom, it manifests his goodness and beneficence.

Thirdly—That the moral duty of man consists in imitating the moral goodness and beneficence of God manifested in the creation towards all his creatures. That seeing, as we daily do, the goodness of God to all men, it is an example calling upon all men to practice the same towards each other; and consequently that everything of persecution and revenge between man and man, and everything of cruelty to animals is a violation of moral duty.

I trouble not myself about the manner of future existence. I content myself with believing, even to positive conviction, that the power that gave me existence is able to continue it in any form and manner he pleases, either with or without this body; and it appears more probable to me that I shall continue to exist hereafter than that I should have had existence, as I now have, before that existence began.

It is certain that in one point all nations of the earth and all religions agree. All believe in a God. The things in which they disagree are the redundancies annexed to that belief; and, therefore, if ever a universal religion should prevail, it will not be believing anything new, but in getting rid of redundancies and believing as man believed at first. Adam, if ever there was such a man, was created a Deist; but in the meantime let every man follow, as he has a right to do, the religion and the worship he prefers. . . .

*   *   *

Revolutionary Times

The American Revolution—the circumstances leading up to it, the war itself, and the events that flowed from it—served as a catalyst to the development of religious freedom. The spirit of individualism, rebellion, and freedom, along with the natural rights and principles of the Declaration of Independence, not only promoted political liberty but also affected religion. Persecution, overt discrimination, or interference with an individual's beliefs, no matter what they were, could no longer be justified. It became apparent that intolerance would have a restraining effect upon the social and economic development of the new society that was coming into being. The spirit of the times also brought on a proliferation of denominations and sects, at the same time that it caused the vast majority of people, although personally religious, not to join any church.

At the same time that the movement toward political freedom encouraged religious liberty, the growth of noncomformity and independence in religion was an important factor in advancing these forces in the political realm.

More than a quarter of a century before the Declaration of Independence, a voice cried out against political tyranny and reminded the American people that the only course for the oppressed was revolution. The voice came from the Boston clergyman Jonathan Mayhew, the author of an earlier selection reprinted here. The occasion was the 100th anniversary of the execution of Charles I by the English people, 1749. His sermon, *A Discourse Concerning Unlimited Submission and Non-Resistance to the Higher Powers,* may have been a generation before its time, but its time did come. What is Mayhew's view of the divine right of kings? How does he base his political convictions on religious principles? How do his arguments in the "Note" draw upon the natural-rights philosophy of John Locke. How are they more radical than Locke's?

A Discourse Concerning Unlimited Submission
Jonathan Mayhew

If we calmly consider the nature of the thing itself, nothing can well be imagined more directly contrary to common sense, than to suppose that *millions* of people should be subjected to the arbitrary, precarious pleasure of *one single man;* (who has *naturally* no superiority over them in point of authority) so that their estates, and every thing that is valuable in life, and even their lives also, shall be absolutely at his disposal, if he happens to be wanton and capricious enough to demand them. What unprejudiced man can think, that God made ALL to be thus subservient to the lawless pleasure and frenzy of ONE, so that it shall always be a sin to resist him! Nothing but the most plain and express revelation from heaven could make a sober impartial man believe such a monstrous, unaccountable doctrine, and, indeed, the thing itself, appears so shocking—so out of all *proportion,* that it may be questioned, whether all the *miracles* that ever were wrought, could make it credible, that this doctrine *really* came from God. At present, there is not the least syllable in scripture which gives any countenance to it. The hereditary, indefeasible, divine right of kings, and the doctrine of nonresistance, which is built upon the supposition of such a right, are altogether as fabulous and chimerical, as transsubstantiation; or any of the most absurd reveries of ancient or modern visionaries. These notions are fetched neither from divine revelation, nor human reason; and if they are derived from neither of these sources, it is not much matter *from whence they come, or whither they go.* Only it is a pity that such doctrines should be propagated in society, to raise factions and rebellions, as we see they have, in fact, been both in the *last,* and in the *present,* REIGN.

But then, if unlimited submission and passive obedience to the *higher powers,* in all possible cases, be not a duty, it will be asked, "How far are we obliged to submit? If we may innocently disobey and resist in some cases, why not in all? Where shall we stop? What is the measure of our duty? This doctrine tends to the total dissolution of civil government; and to introduce such scenes of wild anarchy and confusion, as are more fatal to society than the worst tyranny."

After this manner, some men object; and, indeed, this is the most plausible thing that can be said in favor of such an absolute submission as they plead for. But the worst (or rather the best) of it, is, that there is very little strength or solidity in it. For similar difficulties may be raised with respect to almost every duty of natural and revealed religion.—To instance only in two, both of which are near akin, and indeed exactly parallel, to the case before us. It is unquestionably the duty of children to submit to their parents; and of servants, to their masters. But no one asserts, that it is their duty to obey, and submit to them, in all supposable cases; or universally a sin to resist them. Now does this tend to subvert the just authority of parents and masters? Or to introduce confusion and anarchy into private families? No. How then does the same principle tend to unhinge the government of that larger family, the body politic? We know, in general, that children and servants are obliged to obey their parents and masters respectively. We know also, with equal certainty, that they are not obliged to submit to them in all things, without exception; but may, in some cases, reasonably, and therefore innocently, resist them. These principles are acknowledged upon all hands, whatever difficulty there may be in fixing the exact limits of submission. Now there is at least as much difficulty in stating the measure of duty in these two cases, as in the case of rulers and subjects. So that this is really no objection, at least no reasonable one, against resistance to the *higher powers:* Or, if it is one, it will hold equally against resistance in the other cases mentioned.—It is indeed true, that turbulent, vicious-minded men, may take occasion from this principle, that their rulers may, in some cases, be lawfully resisted, to raise factions and disturbances in the state; and to make resistance where resistance is needless, and therefore, sinful. But is it not equally true, that children and servants of turbulent, vicious minds, may take occasion from this principle, that parents and masters may, in some cases be lawfully resisted, to resist when resistance is unnecessary, and therefore, criminal? Is the principle in either case false in itself, merely because it may be abused; and applied to legitimate disobedience and resistance in those instances, to which it ought not to be applied? According to this way of arguing, there will be no true principles in the world; for there are none but what may be wrested and perverted to serve bad purposes, either through the weakness or wickedness of men. [SEE NOTE.]

A PEOPLE, really oppressed to a great degree by their sovereign, cannot well be insensible when they are so oppressed. And such a people (if I may allude to an ancient *fable*) have, like the *hesperian* fruit, a DRAGON for their *protector* and *guardian:* Nor would they have any reason to mourn, if some HERCULES should appear to dispatch him—For a nation thus abused to arise unanimously, and to resist their prince, even to the dethroning him, is not criminal; but a reasonable way of vindicating their liberties and just rights; it is making use of the means, and the only means, which God has put into their power, for mutual and self-defence. And it would be highly criminal in them, not to make use of this means. It would be stupid tameness, and unaccountable folly, for whole nations to suffer *one* unreasonable, ambitious and cruel man, to wanton and riot in their misery. And in such a case it would, of the two, be more rational to suppose, that they that did NOT *resist,* than that they who did, would *receive to themselves damnation.*

[*Note*] We may very safely assert these two things in general, without undermining government: One is, That no civil rulers are to be obeyed when they enjoin things that are inconsistent with the commands of God: All such disobedience is lawful and glorious; particularly, if persons refuse to comply with any illegal establishment of religion, because it is a gross perversion and corruption (as to doctrine, worship and discipline) of a pure and divine religion, brought from heaven to earth by the *Son of God,* (the only King and Head of the *Christian* church) and propagated through the world by his inspired apostles. All commands running counter to the declared will of the supreme legislator of heaven and earth, are null and void: And therefore disobedience to them is a duty, not a crime. . . . Another thing that may be asserted with equal truth and safety, is, That no government is to be submitted to, at the expense of that which is the *sole end* of all government,—the common good and safety of society. Because, to submit in this case, if it should ever happen, would evidently be to set up the *means* as more valuable, and above, the *end:* than which there cannot be a greater solecism and contradiction. The only reason of the institution of civil government; and the only rational ground of submission to it, is the common safety and utility. If therefore, in any case, the common safety and utility would not be promoted by submission to government, but the contrary, there is no ground or motive for obedience and submission. . . .

Whoever considers the nature of civil government must, indeed, be sensible that a great degree of *implicit confidence,* must unavoidably be placed in those that bear rule: this is implied in the very notion of authority's being originally a *trust,* committed by the people, to those who are vested with it, as all just and righteous authority is; all besides, is mere lawless force and usurpation; neither God nor nature, having given any man a right of dominion over any society, independently of that society's approbation, and consent to be governed by him—Now as all men are fallible, it cannot be supposed that the public affairs of any state, should be always administered in the best manner possible, even by persons of the greatest wisdom and integrity. Nor is it sufficient to legitimate disobedience to the *higher powers* that they are not so administered; or that they are, in some instances, very ill-managed; for upon this principle, it is scarcely supposable that any government at all could be supported, or subsist. Such a principle manifestly tends to the dissolution of government; and to throw all things into confusion and anarchy.—But it is equally evident, upon the other hand, that those in authority may abuse their *trust* and power *to such a degree,* that neither the law of reason, nor of religion, requires, that any obedience or submission should be paid to them; but, on the contrary, that they should be totally *discarded;* and the authority which they were before vested with, transferred to others, who may exercise it more to those good purposes for which it is given . . . . It does not appear but that mankind, in general, have a disposition to be as submissive and passive and tame under government as they ought to be.—Witness a great, if not the greatest, part of the known world, who are now groaning, but not murmuring, under the heavy yoke of tyranny! While those who govern, do it with any tolerable degree of moderation and justice, and, in any good measure act up to their office and character, by being public benefactors; the people will generally be easy and peaceable; and be rather inclined to flatter and adore, than to insult and resist, them. Nor was there ever any *general* complaint against any administration, *which lasted long,* but what there was good reason for. Till people find themselves greatly abused and oppressed by their governors, they are not apt to complain; and whenever they do, in fact, find themselves thus abused and oppressed, they must be stupid not to complain. To say that subjects in general are not proper judges when their governors oppress them, and play the tyrant; and when they defend their rights, administer justice impartially, and promote the public welfare, is as great *treason* as ever man uttered;— 'tis treason,—not against one *single* man, but the state—against the whole body politic;—'tis treason against mankind;—'tis treason against common sense;—'tis treason against God. . . .

*   *   *

The impact that religion made on the nascent spirit of democracy during the Revolutionary period, more specifically the contribution of individual churches to the development of individual liberty, is described in the following selection, one of the few not contemporary to the period with which it deals. Written by Clinton Rossiter, who at the time was chairman of the department of political science of Cornell University, *Seedtime of the Republic* (1953) is a superb analysis of American life on the eve of the Revolution. The passage is from the chapter, "Contributions of Particular Churches to Religious and Political Liberty." In what ways did the Friends have an important bearing on the development of American democracy? Compare the contributions of the Baptists and the Presbyterians. Why were the characteristics of the Anglican Church in the colonies significant in the development of American liberty? Why does Rossiter compare the Catholics then to the Communists in recent times, and what does he mean when he refers to them as "the acid test of the good intentions of the new Republic"?

Seedtime of the Republic

Clinton Rossiter

Of all the churches and sects that gained a hold in the American colonies, five or six proved popular and steadfast enough to work visible effects upon the spirit and institutions of the rising democracy. The contributions of each of the most prominent churches should be briefly noted.

Quakers and Liberty. The Society of Friends was a force to be reckoned with in the social and political life of almost every colony. From the founding of their sect the Quakers of old England looked to the west for a refuge from persecution. Although the hopes of many leaders for a general triumph of Quaker principles in the colonies came to nothing, the ideas and methods of this most persecuted of Christian faiths helped prepare the ground for liberty.

The doctrines of the Quakers were democratic to the core, emphasizing brotherly love, mutual aid and comfort, pacifism, justice for all on equal terms, rejection of priestly authority, and complete religious individualism. The good Quaker, who centered his worldly thoughts upon the problem of individual conduct, would have denied that he possessed any particular theories of state and government. Yet since democracy is simply the presence of a certain number of democrats, and since the good democrat believes in principles that the Quakers put first in their catalogue of virtues, it is plain that the teachings of this sect gave substance to the growing theory of political liberty.

In practice, colonial Quakers aided the cause of liberty in several ways: their meetings were a prime example of democracy in being; they gave the rising nation its only real martyrs to religious persecution in colonial America and fought out of principle for liberty of conscience and abolition of establishments; they provided in Pennsylvania, thanks to the rare nobility of William Penn, a "free colony for all mankind," one of the few areas in the colonies unstained by actual persecution; they took the lead, thanks to the even rarer nobility of John Woolman, in the movement against slavery; and they had easily the best colonial record in dealings with the Indians. The colonies in which they shared or held the reins of political power—Rhode Island, Pennsylvania, early New Jersey, early North Carolina—were some of the most democratic in the colonial period. . . .

Baptists and Liberty. Baptists were in the colonies almost from the beginning. Until well into the eighteenth century, however, they were few, scattered, and friendless, and were persecuted severely in Massachusetts. As late as 1740, long after toleration had been finally secured, only about twenty Baptist congregations could be found in New England, half of these in Rhode Island.

In the meantime, Baptists were flourishing in the middle colonies. Friendly Philadelphia became the center of American Baptism, and from here and the British Isles the church spread its gospel and influence into Virginia and the Carolinas. The Great Awakening had more influence on the Baptists than on any other church, and the growth of this persuasion in the years just before the Revolution was nothing short of astounding. It was a long journey from Rhode Island in 1639 to Virginia in 1776, from the twelve friends of Roger Williams to the enthusiastic horde that outnumbered the Anglicans, and one of deep significance for religious and political liberty.

The Baptists were Calvinist in theology and independent in church polity, differing in doctrine from New England Puritanism only in their opposition to infant baptism and to union of church and state. Their doctrine was basically illiberal and their zeal often rudely excessive. This was especially true of the Separate Baptists, who poured into Virginia and the Carolinas in the third quarter of the eighteenth century. Yet their form of church government, which emphasized the compact, equality, and congregational autonomy, nourished the growth of republican notions, as more than one royal governor acknowledged with his policy of persecution. The organization of the Baptists was more important than their theology, and their organization was as democratic as any in colonial America. Said an early historian of the Baptists, "Our religious education agrees with, and perfectly corresponds with, a government by the people."

American democracy will always be indebted to the colonial Baptists for their singleminded devotion to complete religious liberty. . . . Where most other churches sought freedom within the law, the Baptists would not be satisfied until all laws on religion had been swept away completely.

Presbyterians and Liberty. The history of the Presbyterian Church in colonial America is largely a history of that extraordinary multitude of eighteenth-century immigrants, the Scotch-Irish. . . . The great wave of migration from Ulster to America, which began around 1710 and lasted through the Revolution, spread Scotch-Irish Presbyterianism through all the colonies, especially into the back country from Pennsylvania to the Carolinas. Puritans outside New England entered in strength into this great advancing front of Calvinism and individualism. The first synod was formed at Philadelphia in 1716.

The contributions of the Presbyterians to the rise of colonial liberty were not quite so forceful as those of the Baptists. In both theology and organization they were a good deal more autocratic than several other prominent churches. Yet these points are certainly worth considering: their traditional emphasis on covenant and compact; their efforts to maintain a learned ministry, which led to the establishment of several colleges; the receptivity of the clergy, which was widely devoted to the Scotch philosophy of common sense, to the ideas of the Enlightenment; their activities for toleration, however much in their own interest; . . . and the severe social disruption, the struggle between New Sides and Old Sides, that resulted from the Great Awakening. Most important of all was the unusual fact that the Scotch-Irish were generally more democratic in politics and social attitudes than in religion. In colonial Presbyterianism the stream of democracy flowed in a reverse course. Many a staunch radical in politics was a staunch conservative in religion; many a Scotch-Irish frontiersman moved from an original faith in political man to a more liberal point of view on the possibilities of universal salvation.

Pietism and Liberty. The German Pietist sects—Mennonites, Moravians, Schwenkfelders, Dunkers, and other groups—formed a small but vital religious element in Pennsylvania and scattered localities to the south. The common feature of these groups was their literal devotion, with the usual sectarian shadings, to the tenets of primitive Christianity: dominance of the inner spirit, individual judgment, freedom of conscience, informal worship, sovereignty of the congregation (indeed of each individual who made it up), and often some form of pacifism. All these essentially democratic principles have obvious counterparts in libertarian political theory. Although the Pietists stood aloof from the push-and-pull of colonial politics, the sincerity and simplicity of their methods were yet another support to the upbuilding of American liberty.

Anglicanism and Liberty. It is impossible to make a case for orthodox Anglicanism as a force for colonial liberty, except for the lefthanded manner in which its intolerance of dissent forced dissenters to redouble their efforts for toleration. An intriguing example of Anglican action that ended up producing a libertarian reaction was the eighteenth-century movement—a weak movement at that—for an American bishop. The cause of political independence prospered noticeably from the outcry of opposition to this "Popish plot," and at least some of the outcry burst from Anglican throats.

Nevertheless, the development of the Anglican Church in the Southern colonies provides a convincing case-study of the liberalizing, or perhaps simply enfeebling, effects of the American environment on religious orthodoxy. For a variety of reasons—for example, the fact that no Bishop of London (in whose see [jurisdiction] the colonies were included) ever visited America—colonial Anglicanism was a sorry example of a supposedly hierarchical church. . . .

The pattern of evolution of colonial Anglicanism was that of an aristocratic, hierarchical religion growing ever more congregational in organization and rationalist in doctrine. Although for the most part the churches remained supporters of the conservative party, and although many ministers would have no truck with the patriot cause, Anglicanism passed through the Revolution into its Episcopalian phase without too much disruption or loss of continuity. This pillar of English orthodoxy was decisively Americanized in the colonial period. . . . Fully half the signers of the Declaration of Independence were at least nominal Anglicans.

Jews, Catholics, and Liberty. The influence of these two great and ancient religions, which were later to have such an impact on American life, was hardly noticeable in the colonial period. The small numbers of Jews and slightly larger numbers of Catholics who trickled into the colonies through all this time existed so precariously and anonymously as to leave precious few lasting traces. Jews may take pride in the influence of the Hebraic tradition on the development of American democracy, but must acknowledge that this tradition was fed into the colonies by other hands than those of Israel. Catholics may take pride in the part played by their forefathers in the celebrated Maryland Act of Toleration (1649), but must acknowledge that this law is the most clear-cut instance in colonial history of toleration secured by religionists—Puritans and Catholics—who believed in toleration not at all. . . .

As to the eighteenth century, perhaps the less said the better. Still, it is good and humbling for modern Americans, Catholics as well as Protestants, to recall the difficulties of Catholicism in the generations before the Revolution. Of physical suffering there was little if any, for the policy of almost every colony was much simpler than that: exclusion. . . .

The Catholic occupied much the same position in colonial America that the Communist does today. Though few colonists had ever seen or could have recognized a real live Catholic, they knew everything about "the Papists" and shared a morbid interest in their doctrine and practice. They were also quick to brand people Papists who were not Papists at all. The press found Catholicism excellent copy, especially if the "facts" were bloody or erotic, and especially in times of war with Catholic countries. Certainly the Catholic was feared and despised with the same unthinking passion as is the Communist today, and he was therefore the acid test of the good intentions of the new Republic. The speed with which disqualifications were erased from state laws and constitutions was, considering the heritage of hate and fear, a stunning triumph of reason and democracy. On the eve of the Revolution mass was celebrated publicly only in easy-going Pennsylvania. On the morrow it was celebrated in every state.

*   *   *

The Revolution itself provided a significant impetus to the development of religious liberty. The Anglican Church, which had been established in a number of colonies, was now identified with royal tyranny, and many Anglicans, especially among the upper classes, remained Loyalist. Numbers of opposing sects more generally belonged to the lower classes, which tended to support the Patriot cause. Thus, these denominations were provided with a new worthiness, and religious heterodoxy became respectable for the first time. Furthermore, the physical destruction of church properties by the war accompanied by the social ferment growing out of revolution made it easier to supplant established institutions and introduce innovation, variety, and new freedoms.

By the end of the Revolutionary period, most states had written new constitutions and incorporated in them bills of rights which further reduced state-church ties. Full disestablishment in all states, however, did not come until the middle third of the 19th century. However, there was always the possibility of one state or another reimposing some minor restriction upon those whose religion differed from those of the majority. Nevertheless, unlike the states, the federal government began without an established church, and certainly there was no place where an individual could not worship as he saw fit without fear of persecution.

Achieving the Goal

Virginia was the only state to establish complete religious freedom. The principal reason it became the first state, not only in the United States but in the entire world, to establish complete religious liberty on a firm legal basis was Thomas Jefferson. In 1776, while he was drafting the Declaration of Independence, he gave some of his thought to composing a constitution for his beloved Virginia. It included the article: "All persons shall have full and free liberty of religious opinion; nor shall any be compelled to frequent or maintain any religious institution." A ten-year struggle ensued before Jefferson and his supporters were able to pass this article. They were joined in the effort by dissenting sects, particularly the Baptists, and Jefferson's close friend and political ally, James Madison, who led the fight in the Virginia Assembly. The debates held in that body over church-state relationships were to have a profound effect upon the shaping of the doctrine of religious liberty for the nation as a whole. The final adoption of the Statute of Religious Liberty in 1786 preceded the Constitutional Convention by just one year, at which the delegates from Virginia, with its principles fresh in mind, were to play a prominent role.

When Jefferson in his later years composed the epitaph he wished to have appear on his tombstone, a practice of those times, he did not choose to be remembered for any high office he held: president, vice president, governor, ambassador, or member of the Continental Congress. Instead, he selected three contributions: author of the Declaration of Independence, founder of the University of Virginia, and author of the following selection. Why does he assert that it is wrong for a person to be required to support a church, even one in which he believes? What should be the relation between an individual's religion and his civil rights? What are Jefferson's views on freedom of thought? Why is he convinced that truth will triumph over error?

An Act for Establishing Religious Freedom
Thomas Jefferson

SECTION I. Whereas Almighty God hath created the mind free; that all attempts to influence it by temporal punishments or burthens, or by civil incapacitations, tend only to beget habits of hypocrisy and meanness, and are a departure from the plan of the Holy Author of our religion, who being Lord both of body and mind, yet chose not to propagate it by coercions on either, as was in his Almighty power to do; that the impious presumption of Legislators and rulers, civil as well as ecclesiastical, who being themselves but fallible and uninspired men, have assumed dominion over the faith of others, setting up their own opinions and modes of thinking as the only true and infallible, and as such endeavouring to impose them on others, hath established and maintained false religions over the greatest part of the world; and through all time; that to compel a man to furnish contributions of money for the propagation of opinions which he disbelieves, is sinful and tyrannical; that even the forcing him to support this or that teacher of his own religious persuasion, is depriving him of the comfortable liberty of giving his contributions to the particular pastor, whose morals he would make his pattern, and whose powers he feels most persuasive to righteousness, and is withdrawing from the ministry those temporary rewards, which proceeding from an approbation of their personal conduct, are an additional incitement to earnest and unremitting labors for the instruction of mankind; that our civil rights have no dependence on our religious opinions, any more than our opinions in physics or geometry; that therefore the proscribing any citizen as unworthy the public confidence, by laying upon him an incapacity of being called to the offices of trust and emolument, unless he profess or renounce this or that religious opinion, is depriving him injuriously of those privileges and advantages to which in common with his fellow-citizens he has a natural right; that it tends only to corrupt the principles of that religion it is meant to encourage, by bribing with a monopoly of worldly honors and emoluments, those who will externally profess and conform to it; that though indeed these are criminal who do not withstand such temptation, yet neither are those innocent who lay the bait in their way; that to suffer the civil Magistrate to intrude his powers into the field of opinion, and to restrain the profession or propagation of principles on supposition of their ill tendency, is a dangerous fallacy, which at once destroys all religious liberty, because he being of course judge of that tendency will make his opinions the rule of judgment, and approve or condemn the sentiments of others only as they shall square with or differ from his own; that it is time enough for the rightful purposes of civil government, for its officers to interfere when principles break out into overt acts against peace and good order; and finally, that truth is great and will prevail if left to herself, that she is the proper and sufficient antagonist to error, and has nothing to fear from the conflict, unless by human interposition disarmed of her natural weapons, free argument and debate, errors ceasing to be dangerous when it is permitted freely to contradict them:

SECT. II. *BE it enacted by the General Assembly,* That no man shall be compelled to frequent or support any religious worship, place, or Ministry whatsoever, nor shall be enforced, restrained, molested, or burthened in his body or goods, nor shall otherwise suffer on account of his religious opinions or belief; but that all men shall be free to profess, and by argument to maintain, their opinions in matters of religion, and that the same shall in no wise diminish, enlarge, or affect their civil capacities.

SECT. III. AND though we well know this Assembly elected by the people for the ordinary purposes of legislation only, have no power to restrain the Acts of succeeding Assemblies, constituted with powers equal to our own, and that therefore to declare this Act to be irrevocable, would be of no effect in law; yet we are free to declare, and do declare, that the rights hereby asserted, are of the natural rights of mankind, and that if any Act shall be hereafter passed to repeal the present, or to narrow its operation, such Act will be an infringement of natural right.

*   *   *

Five years passed between the Virginia Statute of Religious Liberty and the ratification of the First Amendment. In the interval, the original Constitution of 1787 was adopted. No mention of God or Creator appears in it. The only reference to religion is a negative one which appears in Article VI, paragraph 3: "No religious Test shall ever be required as a Qualification to any Office or public Trust under the United States." The purpose of this provision was to unequivocally prohibit the imposition of anything comparable to the infamous "test oath" that scarred English history.

The adoption of the First Amendment added the following safeguards: "Congress shall make no law respecting an establishment of religion, or prohibiting the free exercise thereof." These two clauses, the "establishment clause" and the "free exercise clause" state the essence of religious liberty in the United States. The first forbids union of church and state; the second guarantees freedom of conscience. They are like two sides of a coin or two facets of an object, one depending upon and reinforcing the other.

The establishment clause was included to do more than guarantee freedom of thought and practice for dissenting sects; it deprived the state of its customary orthodox support in the suppression of political and cultural experimentation. To Roger Williams disestablishment was the means by which religion would be protected from domination or even interference by the state. To Jefferson, it was the means by which the church could not impose itself on the state. One specific purpose of combining the two clauses together was to ensure that religion would not be used as a basis for classification for purposes of state action, neither for the granting of privileges nor for the infliction of penalties or obligations. No American—whether affiliated with a religious denomination, independent, or nonbelieving—has special standing, may be shown preference in political affairs, or can exert special influence in determining the spiritual values of society. Each has equal status.

Another 77 years passed before the Fourteenth Amendment was added in 1868. It contains no specific mention of religion, but its purpose, as expressed by a member of Congress at the time of its adoption, was to protect by national law the privileges and immunities of all citizens and the inherent rights of all persons against abridgement by unconstitutional actions of any state. In 1879, the Supreme Court declared that the Fourteenth Amendment was a protection of religious liberty. However, not until 1940 in *Cantwell v. Connecticut* did the Court rule that religious liberty was fundamental liberty and that the First Amendment protection was fully extended against the states via the Fourteenth Amendment. This was of major consequence since violations occur more frequently on the state than on the federal level.

The familiar phrase which for most people expresses the essence of church-state relations—"a wall of separation between Church and State"—does not, of course, appear in any part of the Constitution. It was first enunciated by Jefferson in 1801 in a letter to the Danbury Baptists Association, which read in part:

> Believing with you that religion is a matter which lies solely between man and his God, that he owes account to none other for his faith or his worship, that the legislative powers of the Government reach actions only, and not opinions,—I contemplate with sovereign reverence that act of the

whole American people which declared that their legislature should "make no law respecting an establishment of religion, or prohibiting the free exercise thereof," thus building *a wall of separation between Church and State.* [emphasis added]

Although the Supreme Court ultimately adopted this sweeping expression, this does not mean that the issues of church-state relations have become any more easily resolved. Sweeping slogans or broad absolutes do not help to untangle the complex and controversial problems facing American society. Before these problems can be examined, the development of religious liberty in the United States needs to be further unfolded.

Questions

1. How did religion serve as one of the causes of the American Revolution?
2. Did the state in which you live ever have religious qualifications for voting? If so, when were they eliminated?
3. How are the beliefs that Jefferson expresses in *An Act for Establishing Religious Freedom* consistent with those of his *First Inaugural Address.*
4. What became of the Puritans, Anglicans, Pietists, and Deists after the American Revolution?
5. What provisions for religious liberty are established in your state's constitution?

Suggested Readings

The struggle for religious freedom in early America is presented in:

Bates, E. S. *American Faith: Political and Economic Foundations.* New York: W. W. Norton & Co., 1940.

Cobb, Sanford. *The Rise of Religious Liberty in America.* New York, 1902 (DaCapo Press Reprint).

Howe, Mark. *The Garden and the Wilderness.* Chicago: University of Chicago Press, 1965.

Parsons, Wilfred. *The First Freedom: Considerations on Church and State in the United States.* New York: Declan X. McMullin Co., 1948.

Sweet, William. *Religion in Colonial America.* New York: Charles Scribner's Sons, 1942.

The achievement of religious liberty is examined in:

Cousins, Norman, ed. *"In God We Trust": The Religious Beliefs and Ideas of the American Founding Fathers.* New York: Harper & Brothers, 1958.

Koch, G. Adolph. *Republican Religion: The American Revolution and the Cult of Reason.* New York: Henry Holt & Co., 1933.

Littel, Franklin. *From State Church to Pluralism.* Garden City, N. Y.: Doubleday & Co., 1962.

Nye, Russell. *The Cultural Life of the New Nation 1776–1830.* New York: Harper & Row, 1960.

Rossiter, Clinton. *Seedtime of the Republic.* Ithaca: Cornell University Press, 1953.

4. New Approaches

I have sworn upon the altar of God, eternal hostility against every form of tryanny over the mind of man.

—Thomas Jefferson

The period of revolutionary ferment and constitution making, in addition to launching the American people in new political directions, provided opportunity and motivation for the fullest range of self-expression and experimentation in the religious field, a freedom which has reverberated right to the present. As individuals were unshackled from tradition and old orthodoxies, the human mind searched for new answers to the mysteries of the universe and of man's relation to God and to his fellow men. As the nation developed and was influenced by the burgeoning of science and new technologies, the impact upon religion was very profound. Fundamental doctrines became subject to scrutiny and challenge, and religious institutions had to be modified to meet the new economic and social needs of society.

Within any one period of history the responses were richly varied, and new emphases and directions occurred in each period. Consequently, only representative examples will be examined from the long sweep of the nation's religious development.

Multiplication of Sects

During the Early Republic, there was an upsurge in religious interest. Part of it was a reaction to the Deism and skepticism of the Revolutionary period which resulted in a renewed emotional fervor among certain existing churches. The other part involved a tremendous proliferation of new religious denominations and sects, in almost chain-reaction fashion. Once a congregation broke with its parent church or a portion of a congregation split off from the whole, there seemed to be no end to the fragmentation. The standard historical joke was that as soon as an individual with a new set of religious doctrines could find two others whom he could convert, a new church was formed. This proliferation was stimulated and reinforced by the ever-increasing influx of immigrants, the rise of the working classes, and the opening up of the western frontier.

Before the 18th century ended, but gaining in momentum in the early decades of the next, a religious movement occurred which had its roots in the earlier Great Awakening. This was revivalism. Its greatest impact was made in the new frontier regions of the South and the Midwest and particularly affected the Presbyterian, Methodist, and Baptist churches. Utilizing a militant evangelical form of Christianity preached by itinerant self-appointed circuit riders, revivalism brought religion to the isolated farmers. Once or twice a year, a region experienced a marathon camp-meeting session, some lasting up to several weeks. Attended by thousands of emotionally starved people, who came from many miles around and lived in their wagons or tent cities and were exhorted to repentance by teams of preachers, a camp meeting was an intense religious experience, and a social occasion as well.

Peter Cartwright, although an untrained circuit-riding missionary, like most of those involved in the revivalist movement, was a minister of strong convictions, dedication, and ability. Born in Kentucky and a Methodist, he did most of his preaching in the Midwest. The selection that follows consists of excerpts from the *Autobiography of Peter Cartwright,* an edition of which was published in 1856. How does Cartwright reveal his social biases and beliefs? Can you find an explanation for the "jerks"? What other manifestations take place? Why did revivalism affect certain churches and not others?

Autobiography of Peter Cartwright

From 1801 for years a blessed revival of religion spread through almost the entire inhabited parts of the West, Kentucky, Tennessee, the Carolinas, and many other parts, especially through the Cumberland country. . . . The Presbyterians and Methodists in a great measure united in this work, met together, prayed together, and preached together.

In this revival originated our camp-meetings, and in both these denominations they were held every year, and, indeed, have been ever since, more or less. They would erect their camps with logs or frame them, and cover them with clapboards or shingles. They would also erect a shed, sufficiently large to protect five thousand people from wind and rain, and cover it with boards or shingles; build a large stand, seat the shed, and here they would collect together from forty to fifty miles around, sometimes further than that. Ten, twenty and sometimes thirty ministers, of different denominations, would come together and preach night and day, four or five days together; and, indeed, I have known these camp-meetings to last three or four weeks, and great good resulted from them. I have seen more than a hundred sinners fall like dead men under one powerful sermon, and I have seen and heard more than five hundred Christians all shouting aloud the high praises of God at once; and I will venture to assert that many happy thousands were awakened and converted to God at these camp-meetings. Some sinners mocked, some of the old dry professors opposed, some of the old starched Presbyterian preachers preached against these exercises, but still the work went on and spread almost in every direction, gathering additional force, until our country seemed all coming home to God.

In this great revival the Methodists kept moderately balanced; for we had excellent preachers to steer the ship or guide the flock. But some of our members ran wild, and indulged in some extravagancies that were hard to control.

The Presbyterian preachers and members, not being accustomed to much noise or shouting, when they yielded to it went into great extremes and downright wildness, to the great injury of the cause of God. Their old preachers licensed a great many young men to preach, contrary to their Confession of Faith. The Confession of Faith required their ministers to believe in unconditional election and reprobation, and the unconditional and final perseverance of the saints. But in this revival they, almost to a man, gave up these points of high Calvinism, and preached a free salvation to all mankind. The Westminster Confession required every man, before he could be licensed to preach, to have a liberal education; but this qualification was dispensed with, and a great many fine men were licensed to preach without this literary qualification or subscribing to those high-toned doctrines of Calvinism. . . .

In this revival, usually termed in the West the Cumberland revival, many joined the different Churches, especially the Methodist and Cumberland Presbyterians. The Baptists also came in for a share of the converts, but not to any great extent. Infidelity quailed before the mighty power of God, which was displayed among the people. Universalism was almost driven from the land. The Predestinarians of almost all sorts put forth a mighty effort to stop the work of God.

Just in the midst of our controversies on the subject of the powerful exercises among the people under preaching, a new exercise broke out among us, called the *jerks,* which was overwhelming in its effects upon the bodies and minds of the people. No matter whether they were saints or sinners, they would be taken under a warm song or sermon, and seized with a convulsive jerking all over, which they could not by any possibility avoid, and the more they resisted the more they jerked. If they would not strive against it and pray in good earnest, the jerking would usually abate. I have seen more than five hundred persons jerking at one time in my large congregations. Most usually persons taken with the jerks, to obtain relief, as they said, would rise up and dance. Some would run, but could not get away. Some would resist; on such the jerks were generally very severe.

To see those proud young gentlemen and young ladies dressed in their silks, jewelry, and prunella, from top to toe, take the *jerks,* would often excite my risibilities. The first jerk or so, you would see their fine bonnets, caps, and combs fly; and so sudden would be the jerking of the head that their long loose hair would crack almost as loud as a wagoner's whip.

At one of my appointments in 1804 there was a very large congregation turned out to hear the Kentucky boy, as they called me. Among the rest there were two very finely-dressed, fashionable young ladies, attended by two brothers with loaded horse-whips. Although the house was large, it was crowded. The two young ladies, coming in late, took their seats near where I stood, and their two brothers stood in the door. I was a little unwell, and I had a phial of peppermint in my pocket. Before I commenced preaching I took out my phial and swallowed a little of the peppermint. While I was preaching, the congregation was melted into tears. The two young gentlemen moved off to the yard fence, and both the young ladies took the jerks, and they were greatly mortified about it. There was a great stir in the congregation. Some wept, some shouted, and before our meeting closed several were converted.

As I dismissed the assembly a man stepped up to me, and warned me to be on my guard, for he had heard the two brothers swear they would horsewhip me when meeting was out, for giving their sisters the jerks. "Well," said I, "I'll see to that."

I went out and said to the young men that I understood they intended to horsewhip me for giving their sisters the jerks. One replied that he did. I undertook to expostulate with him on the absurdity of the charge against me, but he swore I need not deny it; for he had seen me take out a phial, in which I carried some truck that gave his sisters the jerks. As quick as thought it came into my mind how I would get clear of my whipping, and, jerking out the peppermint phial, said I, "Yes; if I gave your sisters the jerks I'll give them to you." In a moment I saw he was scared. I moved toward him, he backed, I advanced, and he wheeled and ran, warning me not to come near him, or he would kill me. It raised the laugh on him, and I escaped my whipping. I had the pleasure, before the year was out, of seeing all four soundly converted to God, and I took them into the Church.

While I am on this subject I will relate a very serious circumstance which I knew to take place with a man who had the jerks at a camp-meeting, on what was called the Ridge, in William Magee's congregation. There was a great work of religion in the encampment. The jerks were very prevalent. There was a company of drunken rowdies who came to interrupt the meeting. These rowdies were headed by a very large drinking man. They came with their bottles of whisky in their pockets. This large man cursed the jerks, and all religion. Shortly afterward he took the jerks, and he started to run, but he jerked so powerfully he could not get away. He halted among some saplings, and, although he was violently agitated, he took out his bottle of whisky, and swore he would drink the damned jerks to death; but he jerked at such a rate he could not get the bottle to his mouth, though he tried hard. At length he fetched a sudden jerk, and the bottle struck a sapling and was broken to pieces, and spilled his whisky on the ground. There was a great crowd gathered round him, and when he lost his whisky he became very much enraged, and cursed and swore very profanely, his jerks still increasing. At length he fetched a very violent jerk, snapped his neck, fell, and soon expired, with his mouth full of cursing and bitterness.

I always looked upon the jerks as a judgment sent from God, first, to bring sinners to repentance; and, secondly, to show professors that God could work with or without means, and that he could work over and above means, and do whatsoever seemeth him good, to the glory of his grace and the salvation of the world.

There is no doubt in my mind that, with weak-minded, ignorant, and superstitious persons, there was a great deal of sympathetic feeling with many that claimed to be under the influence of this jerking exercise; and yet, with many, it was perfectly involuntary. It was, on all occasions, my practice to recommend fervent prayer as a remedy, and it almost universally proved an effectual antidote.

There were many other strange and wild exercises into which the subjects of this revival fell; such, for instance, as what was called the running, jumping, barking exercise. The Methodist preachers generally preached against this extravagant wildness. I did it uniformly in my little ministrations, and sometimes gave great offense; but I feared no consequences when I felt my awful responsibilities to God. From these wild exercises, another great evil arose from the heated and wild imaginations of some. They professed to fall into trances and see visions; they would fall at meetings and sometimes at home, and lay apparently powerless and motionless for days, sometimes for a week at a time, without food or drink; and when they came to, they professed to have seen heaven and hell, to have seen God, angels, the devil and the damned; they would prophesy, and, under the pretense of Divine inspiration, predict the time of the end of the world, and the ushering in of the great millennium.

This was the most troublesome delusion of all; it made such an appeal to the ignorance, superstition, and credulity of the people, even saint as well as sinner. I watched this matter with a vigilant eye. If I opposed it, I would have to meet the clamor of the multitude; and if anyone opposed it, these very visionists would single him out, and denounce the dreadful judgments of God against him. They would even set the very day that God was to burn the world, like the self-deceived modern Millerites. They would prophesy, that if any one did oppose them, God would send fire down from heaven and consume him, like the blasphemous Shakers. They would proclaim that they could heal all manner of diseases, and raise the dead, just like the diabolical Mormons. They professed to have converse with spirits of the dead in heaven and hell, like the modern spirit rappers. Such a state of things I never saw before, and I hope in God I shall never see again. . . .

*   *   *

The multiplication of sects to an extent unknown any place else in the world was an inevitable outgrowth of two factors: the Protestant belief in individual interpretation of Scripture and the freedom that existed in 19th-century America to do something about it. The new denominations took many different forms. Some, following the example of Deism, took a rational approach to the Bible. Either they accepted it as God's Word but dismissed those passages that defied reason, or they rejected it as revelation and sought God in their hearts. From these approaches evolved the Universalists, Unitarians, and the philosophy-religion of Transcendentalism. Others returned to the practices of the early Christians who lived together in communal societies. When Utopian socialism came into vogue during the Jacksonian era, a number of the communities established were formed by religious groups. One of them was Oneida, in New York, founded by the Perfectionists and headed by John Humphrey Noyes. In addition, there were the celibate societies, the most famous being the Shakers founded by "Mother" Ann Lee, and the Rappites named after "Father" George Rapp. Those who opposed the fragmentation of religion organized all-embracing "Christian" churches, which resulted in more sects.

Yet another approach was that of fundamentalism which involved pietism and literal acceptance of the Bible as written. This resulted in the formation of a variety of sects, small in numbers but with unusual beliefs. None were more unusual or more dramatic than the Millennialists, who deduced from Scriptures that the "second coming" of Christ was imminent, or in other words, that the world was about to come to an end. The most well-known of the Millennialists were the followers of William Miller of Vermont. After years of careful analysis of the Bible and intricate calculations, he publicly announced in 1832 that the second coming would occur in 1843 or 1844. As the fateful time approached his following rapidly increased in numbers; one source placed the number at close to a million. The Millerites believed that they, the Saints or true believers, would be drawn up into Heaven when the millennium arrived, whereas everyone else and the world itself would be engulfed in flames of destruction. As the day of judgment drew nearer, some found the strain too much, committing suicide or going insane.

The following selection provides a description, typical enough, of what happened in Philadelphia. It is taken from J. Thomas Scharf and Thompson Westcott, *History of Philadelphia,* published in 1884. What preparation did the Millerites make for the millennium? What was the reaction of nonbelievers? How do you think the adherents felt on that final day? What made the movement possible?

Millerism

J. Thomas Scharf and Thompson Westcott

The excitement in Philadelphia had been growing for two or more years, and by the summer of 1844 it was indescribable. The Millerite Church was on Julianna Street, between Wood and Callowhill, and there Miller's followers met night and day, and watched the stars and sun, and prayed and warned the unrepentant that the "Day of Judgment was at hand."

Many of them began to sell their houses at prices which were merely nominal. Others gave away their personal effects, shut up their business, or vacated their houses. On a store on Fifth Street, above Chestnut, was a placard which read thus:

"This shop is closed in honor of the King of Kings who will appear about the 20th of October. Get ready friends to crown Him Lord of all."
. . . People laboring under the excitement went mad.

On one occasion all the windows of a meeting-house were surrounded at night by a crowd of young fellows, and at a given signal the darkness and gloom were made lurid by flaming torches, and the air resounded with the roar of firecrackers. The Saints inside went wild with terror, for they thought the fiery whirlwind was come.

The Sunday before the final day was an eventful one. The Julianna Street Chapel was crowded. A mob of unbelievers on the pavements stoned the windows and hooted at the worshippers. The police of Northern Liberties, and Spring Garden, and a sheriff's posse, headed by Morton McMichael, were on hand to quell the threatened disturbance. The members of the congregation repaired to their homes, and after, in many cases, leaving their doors and windows open, and giving away their furniture, set out for the suburban districts. A large number went over into New Jersey, but their chief party assembled in Isaac Yocomb's field on the Darby Road, three miles and a half from the Market Street bridge. While here a furious hurricane strengthened the faith of the Millerites and struck awful terror to the souls of the timid. It swept over the city, destroying shipping and demolishing houses. . . .

The crowd at Darby was gathered in two tents, but so great was it that the children for two days were obliged to run about the fields, exposed to the pelting of a pitiless storm, and crying for their parents. The parents, clad in their white ascension robes, were almost exhausted for want of food, slept on the cold wet ground, and prayed and hymned and groaned incessantly.

At midnight on the 22d, the Bridegroom was to come, and a rain of fire was to descend from the heavens, and the Saints were to be gathered up in a whirlwind. There they stood on that black, tempestuous October night, shivering with cold and fear—their faces upturned, and every eye strained to catch a beam of the awful light piercing the clouds. The morning broke, and with it came the end of the delusion. The assemblage dispersed in despair, and slunk away silently and downcast to their houses.

*   *   *

Postscript

When the millennium did not come on the appointed day, many of the followers abandoned the movement. Miller, under pressure, chose another day, with the same result. After this, the movement completely collapsed, and Miller died a few years later a broken man. From the few remaining believers there developed several Adventist sects including the Seventh Day Adventist Church.

Of all the denominations that sprang into being during this time, none suffered more tribulation and violent persecution or had such a significant effect upon the nation's development as did the Church of Jesus Christ of Latter-Day Saints. Its founder was Joseph Smith, a farm boy from Palmyra, New York, who had a vision from God. In 1823, he received a visitation from the angel Moroni who informed him of the existence of golden plates upon which were engraved revelations of God. The plates were translated and published seven years later as the Book of Mormon, and the Church was organized. The Mormons' purpose was to restore Christianity to the form set up by Jesus, and the term "Latter-Day Saints" was designed to distinguish it from the earlier organization. Converts flocked to it with great zeal, but they were persecuted by others. The Mormons were forced to flee from New York to various locations in the Midwest, where they established their communities. In Illinois, in 1844, Smith was killed by a lynch mob, and after two years of fighting, the Mormons' new prophet, Brigham Young, decided to emigrate into the western wilderness. Some 5,000 made the heroic journey to their Deseret or promised land, the barren valley of the Great Salt Lake.

Not only were the Mormons able to establish themselves in one of the most forbidding portions of a region of the United States that was not to be fully developed until a generation later, but they spread their commonwealth in many directions. Through rigid discipline, back-breaking labor, community cooperation, the subsidization of immigration, and irrigation and fertilization which made the desert bloom, they were able to found hundreds of settlements in the Southwest, California, the Northwest, Canada, and Mexico. They then turned to international missionary work. Today, the Mormons number about 1.5 million. They constitute a dynamic, growing religion which emphasizes youth training and service, and their influence in the political, economic, and social life of Utah and several other western states is great.

One aspect of Mormon belief that from the start aroused popular interest, as well as virulent persecution from time to time, was the practice of polygamy. Although one historian maintains that it was introduced by the church elders as a recruitment device and would eventually have become insignificant, Mormon authorities asserted that it was an obligation to be fulfilled whenever possible and failure to do so could result in damnation. Be that as it may, non-Mormons reacted intensely to a practice they felt violated basic morality. Although the pitched battles and lynchings that occurred earlier in the East came to an end, practitioners were subject to arrest for violating laws against bigamy. Ultimately, a case involving the issue reached the Supreme Court. In *Reynolds v. United States* (1878), a conviction for bigamy in the territorial courts of Utah was sustained. Chief Justice Morrison Waite rejected the contention of the defense that to punish Reynolds for acting in conformity with his religious duty was a violation of the "free exercise" clause. While it was true that government could not interfere with religious beliefs and opinions, it could act against conduct which was "in violation of social duties or subversive of good order." Despite the decision, some Mormons refused for a few years longer to forgo the practice. Finally, the church elders agreed to include in the draft constitution of Utah a clear prohibition against polygamy, and Congress in 1890 admitted the territory into the Union as a state.

The Catholic Issue

Although by no means a new denomination or sect, the Roman Catholic Church became significant to American religious history in the early 19th century. Before this, its only effect upon American history, as we have seen, was in the Maryland Toleration Act. At the time the nation was launched, Catholics in the country numbered approximately 35,000, about 1 percent of the total population. Their numbers trebled over the next 30 years, but with the great migrations of Irish and Germans in the middle third of the 19th century, they burgeoned to three million and became larger than any single Protestant denomination. Anti-Catholic prejudice was rekindled. Bigoted tracts appeared, a nativist crusade, as much anti-foreign as anti-Catholic, was launched by the American Protestant Association and the Know-Nothing Party. Irish were denied all but the most menial employment, and mobs attacked and burned a number of convents and churches in the principal cities.

As time went by, these blatant forms of intolerance and discrimination began to wane. The Know-Nothing Movement died just before the Civil

War, the Irish improved their economic position in the postwar era, and
Protestants generally seemed to get over their initial conviction that a "takeover" by the Vatican was imminent. Nevertheless, certain social issues
served to divide the American people on religious lines, a number of which
persist to the present. Some of the more important ones are examined in the
following selection which presents the Catholic position on them. It is taken
from "The Catholic Church," a lecture by John Lancaster Spaulding which
appeared in his book, *Lectures and Discourses,* published in 1882. Bishop
Spaulding taught and wrote extensively on matters of faith and education
and was considered a spokesman for the Roman Catholic Church in America. What is the meaning of each of the marks (characteristics) of the
Church: one, holy, Catholic, and apostolic? How does Bishop Spaulding define liberty and free will? Why does he consider education and, particularly,
religious education so essential? What are his views on secular public
schools, parental responsibility, a denominational system, and parochial education?

The Catholic Church
John Lancaster Spaulding

The Church is one, holy, Catholic, and apostolic. Its essential unity is
derived from the Holy Ghost, who is its principle of life. "What the soul is
to the body," says St. Augustine, "the Spirit of Jesus Christ is to the Church.
He acts in the universal Church as the soul acts in the whole body. A limb
that is cut off dies; life remains in the body, but not in the dissevered member; and so the Holy Ghost does not abide with those who have separated
themselves from the body of the Church." The Church, then, is one in its
principle of life, from which it also derives its unity of organization, of government, of doctrine, and of worship. Opposed to unity are heresy and
schism. Heresy violates unity of doctrine, and schism unity of organization
and government. Doctrinal error, however, may exist without heresy. . . .
Obstinacy in error, leading to rebellion against the teaching authority of the
Church, is heresy, and the obstinacy which results in revolt against its governing power is schism. Since unity is a distinctive mark of the Church, it
follows at once that the whole Catholic system must necessarily rest upon
the principle of authority. It is idle to talk of unity in religion where there is
no supreme and infallible voice to command obedience. This infallible voice
is that of the living Church, which Christ commanded to teach all nations, to
which He promised His unfailing help, to which He sent the Holy Ghost on
the day of Pentecost, to be for all times its guide and unerring teacher. Authority is as essential to the Church as is the Church to the growth and con-
tinuance of Christianity. Authority is the highest social principle. Upon it all
laws rests, and from it all obedience is derived. If the church is a society, it

must necessarily possess authority; if it is a supernatural society it must necessarily possess infallible authority. A book, even though inspired, cannot be the principle of authority in any society. It may be a most serviceable ally and support both of authority and of liberty, just as a written constitution may be a beneficent guide to the legislative and judicial tribunals of the nation; but the national life precedes the documents that contain its theories and principles of government, and it cannot be confined within the limits of a code. In this sense the authority of the Church is higher than that of the New Testament. The Bible is God's infallible word when its true meaning is made known to us by His infallible church; and all other theories concerning its authority will lead to absurdities and contradictions. To make it the supreme rule of faith is equivalent to a denial of the unity of the Church, and, in the last analysis, of the truth of Christianity.

The Catholicity of the Church is the expansion of its unity. Were it not one it could not be Catholic. A distinction must be made between the principle and the fact of Catholicity. As a matter of fact the Church is not universal: nor are we bound to believe that it is ever destined to become so here on earth. It is its fate rather to live in this world in the midst of conflicts, persecutions, struggles, and trials. It waxes strong here, and there it falls into decay; now it triumphs, and in another age it suffers defeat. When it rises in influence, and wealth and honors are heaped upon it, the gain is not unfrequently offset by a weakening of faith and the loss of religious earnestness; and hence it does not seem to enter into the divine plan to lead the Church on to universal sway over all men and all places, though it was founded to teach the whole truth as revealed by Christ to all men and until the end of time. The Church is thus the embodiment of the universal and absolutely true religion; and in principle and of right it is therefore Catholic, even while its diffusion through the earth remains partial and its actual universality but relative. This relative Catholicity, which admits of degrees, is found in the fact that the Church is not confined to one or several countries, but is spread among many nations and counts adherents in almost every part of the world; and thus the one faith, with the one form of worship and government, is brought practically within the reach of all men. The opposites of the note of Catholicity are sectarianism and religious nationalism, which, however, is but a form of sectarianism. The essential holiness of the Church is derived from its principle of life, which is the Holy Ghost. This inward and essential sanctity is made manifest in the power to regenerate men and endow them with higher moral and religious strength. The saints—those in whom the love of God and man attains heroic force—are as a seal upon the Church to witness to its divine origin. They give objective reality and historic sequence to its sanctity.

The essential holiness of the Church is distinct from the accidental holiness conferred upon it by the lives of the saints; and though all who believe were sinners, the Church would still be holy, as God is good though the whole race of men is fallen and perverse. The supernatural supposes nature, and grace does not do violence to free will; and hence the accidental sanctity of the Church is relative and variable. It is not necessary that this or that number of its members should be saints; nor is its holiness diminished by the sinful lives of multitudes of nominal Catholics, since their depravity is the result of their wilful disobedience to its spirit and commandments. Nevertheless, as a matter of fact the race of the saints is never extinguished, and in every age many are found whose heroic virtues testify to the supernatural principle by which their lives are inspired. Faith, hope, and charity, revealed in the immolation of one's self in a life of humility, chastity, and poverty, and sanctioned by special marks of God's favor, discover the saints to us, the chief among whom the Church places in the Canon by a solemn and official pronouncement.

Apostolicity is the fourth note by which the true Church is made known to us. Founded by Christ Jesus on Peter and the apostles, it rises heavenward through the ages as a beacon to all the world. It is to-day, it was yesterday; it is in all the centuries since Christ was born. The other apostolic churches have perished—Antioch, Alexandria, and Jerusalem; Rome alone remains. . . . The transmission of the one Catholic faith from generation to generation is made through a definite and strongly marked channel. The stream rises in the mountain where Christ died, and the priest who to-day in some remote wilderness preaches the Gospel to savages irrigates the barren waste with waters that flow from that fountain-head along historic courses. By this Church, one, Catholic, holy, and apostolic, the world has been converted to Christ. Christians who are separated from its communion descend from ancestors who were baptized in the Catholic faith. As this Church is the organ of Christ, by which His will is made known to men, so is it the channel through which His graces flow to those who are saved. To recognize the true Church by the marks here indicated, and yet to refuse, from whatever motive, to enter its fold, is to deny Christ and to love this life more than that which is eternal. Hence the apothegm, Out of the Church there is no salvation. True Christianity is found in the Church, and not elsewhere. The Church is the form of the religion of Christ, which thus becomes historic, permanent, consistent with itself. It is this organic form which lifts it out of the region of speculation and abstractions and gives to it a concrete existence.

The Church has a threefold office—viz., teaching, sacred ministry, and rule; and hence Christianity, as Cardinal Newman says, is at once a philosophy, a religious rite, and a political power. The office of teaching finds expression in a system of religious doctrines, that of sacred ministry in a form of worship, and that of rule in an ecclesiastical polity. . . .

. . . Liberty and toleration, which enter so largely into the constitution of civil society, especially in our day, cannot be left out of sight when there is question of the relations of Church and state.

Liberty, as Catholics understand the word, is not the right to do whatever one may please to do. This is rather the idea of license, which is the negation of liberty and of society. That man is endowed with free will is a doctrine of the Church and a fact, but the exercise of this faculty should be controlled by reason and by law. Man is free to do evil, but he has not the right to do evil. Hence when there is question of lawful liberty there can be no thought of absolute liberty. Political society is based upon the sacrifice which the individual makes of a portion of his natural freedom, in order that he may thereby secure benefits which are greater than that freedom. Duty is the basis of the moral, and consequently of the social order; and duty is not possible without self-denial, self-conquest. Our duties determine our rights, since we may demand of others only what they are in duty bound to give us. As it is man's duty to obey God, and thereby to attain to his own highest destiny, he has a divine and inalienable right to whatever is necessary to this end; and this right is the foundation and bulwark of all true liberty.

It is from this principle that the spirit of freedom is derived which rebels against the pagan constitution of society, according to which the state has the right to absorb the whole activity of man, to control his private life, to regulate his duties and even his pleasures; and the tendency to attribute to the state a quasi-omnipotence at the expense of the individual, the family, and the Church is invariably an evidence of the decay of Christian faith, as it is also clearly a mark of a servile habit of thought and sentiment. Society which in its principles and morals is faithful to the law of God is worthy to be free; and in such a society the government will make itself felt as little as possible, its action being confined chiefly to enforcing respect for the rights of others and to the maintenance of equilibrium among the social forces. The sense of duty will create the spirit of obedience, and obedience to law, founded in justice and equity, is liberty. As to the liberty of the press and freedom of conscience, it is plain that no society can commit itself to the principle that its exercise should be unhampered by restraint of any kind. With us, for example, the liberty of the press does not extend to the publication of obscene matter, and it is still further restricted by the law of libel; and we do not hold that under the plea of liberty of conscience men should be permitted to practise polygamy or free-love, or offer human sacrifices. All men who are not enemies of society itself must agree that unrestricted liberty is license; and hence differences that may arise between the Church and state on this point will be found to relate, as a rule, to policy and not to principle. Liberty of conscience, when properly defined, is a doctrine which Catholics accept and have always accepted. . . .

Charity and humility tend, as a rule, to make us merciful and tolerant, and hence the Christian religion, which creates these virtues, has been and is the world's great fountain-head of mercy and toleration. But the habit of forbearance and patience, whether with regard to the faults or the opinions of others, must, like all habits, be acquired, and it will therefore be chiefly found in those who are surrounded by influences that are favorable to its cultivation. Where a whole people are united in one faith they will not readily tolerate those who seek to destroy the harmony of religious belief; and if unity is a mark of Christian truth, it is surely not desirable that they should act otherwise. They defend the unity of religious society with the same ardor and with more or less the same weapons with which they defend the unity of the national life when it is attacked. But where men who hold different creeds are intermingled in society they will inevitably end by tolerating one another—if for no other reason, from mere weariness of strife and collision. Again, where men have no religious faith at all they will, as a rule, from sheer indifference, grow to be tolerant. We easily allow free scope to opinions and practices for which we care nothing.

The toleration which exists so widely at present throughout the civilized world is the result of the interaction of many causes. The Christian doctrines concerning the worth of the soul, the inviolability of conscience, the brotherhood of all men, the distinction between Church and state, the duty of charity and justice even to the slave, created, little by little, a social condition in which the spirit of a true and wise tolerance was naturally developed; and this spirit would have continued to grow and diffuse itself with the progress of learning and the refinement of manners, even had the harmony and unity of the Christian religion not been broken by the heresies and schisms of the sixteenth century. The multitude of religions, however, together with the infidelity and indifference which were the inevitable results of this crisis in European history, have, in conjunction with industry and commerce and the more frequent and rapid intercourse made possible by mechanical inventions, greatly accelerated and otherwise modified the movement of the modern nations towards larger liberty and toleration. As to the form of civil government the Church is indifferent, and leaves the people to shape their political constitutions upon monarchical, aristocratic, or democratic principles, according to their customs and preferences.

Whatever the form of government may be, there are interests which concern alike the Church and the state, and which neither, consequently, should be asked to abandon. The question of education at once suggests itself as the most important of these common interests, and the one concerning which conflict of authority has in our day most frequently arisen.

Whoever educates necessarily influences, whether for good or evil, man's whole being. In thought we separate the intellect from the conscience and the soul from the body, but in the living man they are always united, and to develop the one without at the same time acting upon the other is not possible; and hence a school system which professes to eliminate religious and moral truth from the process of education, and to impart secular knowledge alone, commits itself to an impossible task. The thoughts, opinions, sentiments, the morals, laws, and history, of a people are all interpenetrated by and blended with their religious beliefs; and the attempt to eliminate religion from knowledge, sentiment from morality, or the past history of a people from its present life is as absurd as would be the effort to abstract from the character of the man the agencies and influences that wrought upon him in childhood and in youth. As the child is father of the man, so is faith the mother of knowledge; and the deepest and highest form of faith is religious faith. Hence when the state organizes a system of education from which the teaching of religious doctrines is excluded, it fatally, though possibly unconsciously and negatively, commits itself to an irreligious and infidel propagandism; since to ignore religious doctrines while striving to develop the intellectual and moral faculties must result in the gradual extinction of faith, as the disuse of an organ or a faculty superinduces atrophy and gradual disappearance. The plea that the Church is the proper place for religious instruction is not to the point; for, if religion is true or valuable, it must, like the air of heaven, envelop and interpenetrate the whole life of man; and hence to exclude it from the daily, systematic efforts to awaken in the child quicker perception and fuller consciousness is equivalent to a denial of its truth and efficacy; and the practical tendency of such a school system will inevitably lie in the direction of its logical bearing.

Religion, which is the bond between the Creator and the creature, founds, both in idea and in fact, the first society. The first association of human beings, however, both in idea and in fact, is the family, whose essential constitution looks not merely to the propagation of the race, but above all, to its education; since without the family the race might be propagated, while it is not conceivable that without it, it could, in any proper sense, be educated. Hence parents are the natural educators, and any system which tends to weaken their control over their children or interferes with the free exercise of their natural rights is radically vicious. It is therefore the duty of both Church and state to co-operate with the family in the work of education, since when the spirit of the school is in conflict with the spirit which prevails in the child's home, the result must necessarily be an incomplete and inharmonious type of manhood. A state which professes to tolerate different forms of religion contradicts its own principles and becomes intolerant whenever it compels its citizens to support a uniform system of schools. Such a system, if it ignores or excludes all religious instruction, does violence to the consciences of all sincere and thoughtful believers; and if it teaches the tenets of some one creed, it wrongs those of a different faith. Nor is it possible to escape from the difficulty by accepting the beliefs which are common to all. As a matter of fact, in the modern state no such common beliefs exist, since there are sects of atheists, materialists, and pantheists in all countries in which the bond of Christian unity has been broken. But, even if this were not so, beliefs which are common to a multitude of sects are not held in common, but as parts of integral systems which are distinct and unlike, and to separate them from the organism to which they belong is to mutilate them and thereby to deprive them of their true meaning and efficacy.

The state, therefore, which tolerates different forms of religion is thereby debarred from the right to establish a uniform school system; and yet it is unreasonable to ask the state to do nothing to promote and spread education, since, after religion, education is the chief agent of civilization, and, in the absence of governmental aid and supervision, many parents, and ministers of religion even, will either altogether neglect this most important work or at best perform it in an inefficient and careless manner. In a free state, then, where religious tolerance is a fundamental principle of law, the government, in fostering education, is bound to respect scrupulously the rights of the family and liberty of conscience; and this it cannot do, if the schools are supported by taxation, except by instituting what is known as the denominational system of education. The practical difficulties to be overcome are not insuperable; and since there is question here of a fundamental principle of free government, the obstacles to its practical acceptance and enforcement should but serve to inspire just and enlightened statesmen with a more determined will to remove them. If, however, the state should establish a school system from which religion is excluded, it becomes the imperative duty of Catholics to found schools to which they can, with a safe conscience, send their children; and if, instead of doing this, they remain passive, with a sort of vague hope that somehow or other a change for the better will be brought about, they have denied the faith, according to the doctrine of St. Paul: "But if any man have not care of his own, and especially those of his house, he hath denied the faith."

*   *   *

Differences in viewpoint over social issues such as education, censorship, divorce, and birth control between Catholics and those of other faiths served to keep alive the smoldering embers of prejudice. Particularly in rural areas where native Protestants had little or no contact with foreign born and those of other religions, suspicion and animosity persisted. This was especially true in the South, which experienced a revival after World War I of the Ku Klux Klan aimed primarily against Catholics and immigrants. These attitudes came to a head in the 1928 Presidential campaign.

For a generation or more before 1928, Catholics had entered into the mainstream of American political life, as voters, party leaders, and elected officials on local, state, and national levels. But until this time, none had been elected, or even nominated, to the highest office in the land. In 1928, the Democratic Party broke with tradition and nominated Alfred E. Smith, the outstanding progressive Governor of New York and a devout Roman Catholic. From the outset, an insidious, underground "whispering campaign" was carried on against him on the grounds that, as a Catholic, his allegiance would be divided between his country and Rome. Smith tried valiantly to overcome these smear tactics. In an open letter, speaking for his fellow-American co-religionists, he forthrightly defended their religious beliefs and his conviction that they could uphold the Constitution of the United States and the principles of the Republic as loyally as any other citizens, no matter what their faith. But to no avail; the American people were not ready to practice what the First Amendment called for. Historians concur that Smith would have probably lost the election no matter what his religion, but the margin of his defeat was clearly because he was Catholic.

It took another eight Presidential elections for a major party to nominate a Catholic again. This time the electorate responded positively. Of course, John F. Kennedy had certain advantages over his predecessor. Although both were big-city Irish Catholics, Smith had been raised on the sidewalks of New York, had been associated with rough-and-tumble machine politics, and, although well educated, did not sound it. On the other hand, Kennedy was born into a wealthy, almost aristocratic family, was young, handsome, and charming, was educated at Harvard, and was a war hero. More important, this time being a Catholic was an asset. Experts who analyzed the election returns concluded that, on balance, Kennedy's religion gained for him more votes than it lost for him. The American voters came of age.

The following selection is taken from a speech that Kennedy delivered to the Greater Houston Ministerial Association on September 12, 1960. Fully cognizant of the fate of his predecessor, Kennedy chose to meet the issue head-on and examine it before a group of ministers. The address was given wide circulation. How does Kennedy specifically define separation of church and state? What does he conceive of as the religious role of the President? What does he mean by the statement: "I am not a Catholic candidate for President. I am the Democratic party's candidate for President who happens also to be a Catholic"? Why do most Americans feel that Kennedy's election in 1960 marked the fruition of religious liberty in the United States?

Speech to the Greater Houston Ministerial Association
John F. Kennedy

While the so-called religious issue is necessarily and properly the chief topic here tonight, I want to emphasize from the outset that I believe that we have far more critical issues in the 1960 election. . . .

But because I am a Catholic, and no Catholic has ever been elected President, the real issues in this campaign have been obscured—perhaps deliberately, in some quarters less responsible than this. So it is apparently necessary for me to state once again—not what kind of church I believe in, for that should be important only to me, but what kind of America I believe in.

I believe in an America where the separation of church and state is absolute—where no Catholic prelate would tell the President (should he be a Catholic) how to act and no Protestant minister would tell his parishioners for whom to vote—where no church or church school is granted any public funds or political preference—and where no man is denied public office merely because his religion differs from the President who might appoint him or the people who might elect him.

I believe in an America that is neither Catholic, Protestant or Jewish —where no public official either requests or accepts instructions on public policy from the Pope, the National Council of Churches or any other ecclesiastical source—where no religious body seeks to impose its will directly or indirectly upon the general populace or the public acts of its officials—and where religious liberty is so indivisible that an act against one church is treated as an act against all.

For, while this year it may be a Catholic against whom the finger of suspicion is pointed, in other years it has been, and may someday be again, a Jew—or a Quaker—or a Unitarian—or a Baptist. It was Virginia's harassment of Baptist preachers, for example, that led to Jefferson's statute of religious freedom. Today, I may be the victim—but tomorrow it may be you —until the whole fabric of our harmonious society is ripped apart at a time of great national peril.

Finally, I believe in an America where religious intolerance will someday end—where all men and all churches are treated as equal—where every man has the same right to attend or not to attend the church of his choice —where there is no Catholic vote, no anti-Catholic vote, no bloc voting of any kind—and where Catholics, Protestants and Jews, both the lay and the pastoral level, will refrain from those attitudes of disdain and division which have so often marred their works in the past, and promote instead the American ideal of brotherhood.

This is the kind of America in which I believe. And it represents the kind of Presidency in which I believe—a great office that must be neither humbled by making it the instrument of any religious group, nor tarnished by arbitrarily withholding its occupancy from the members of any religious group. I believe in a President whose views on religion are his own private affair, neither imposed upon him by the nation or imposed by the nation upon him as a condition to holding that office.

I would not look with favor upon a President working to subvert the First Amendment's guarantees of religious liberty (nor would our system of checks and balances permit him to do so). And neither do I look with favor upon those who would work to subvert Article VI of the Constitution by requiring a religious test—even by indirection—for if they disagree with that safeguard, they should be openly working to repeal it.

I want a chief executive whose public acts are responsible to all and obligated to none—who can attend any ceremony, service or dinner his office may appropriately require him to fulfill—and whose fulfillment of his Presidential office is not limited or conditioned by any religious oath, ritual or obligation.

This is the kind of America I believe in—and this is the kind of America I fought for in the South Pacific and the kind my brother died for in Europe. No one suggested then that we might have a "divided loyalty," that we did not "believe in liberty" or that we belonged to a disloyal group that threatened "the freedoms for which our forefathers died."

And in fact this is the kind of America for which our forefathers did die when they fled here to escape religious test oaths, that denied office to members of less favored churches, when they fought for the Constitution, the Bill of Rights, the Virginia Statute of Religious Freedom—and when they fought at the shrine I visited today—the Alamo. For side by side with Bowie and Crockett died Fuentes and McCafferty and Bailey and Bedillo and Carey—but no one knows whether they were Catholics or not. For there was no religious test there.

I ask you tonight to follow in that tradition, to judge me on the basis of fourteen years in the Congress—on my declared stands against an ambassador to the Vatican, against unconstitutional aid to parochial schools, and against any boycott of the public schools (which I attended myself)—and instead of doing this do not judge me on the basis of these pamphlets and publications we have all seen that carefully select quotations out of context from the statements of Catholic Church leaders, usually in other countries, frequently in other centuries, and rarely relevant to any situation here—and always omitting of course, that statement of the American bishops in 1948 which strongly endorsed church-state separation.

I do not consider these other quotations binding upon my public acts —why should you? But let me say, with respect to other countries, that I am wholly opposed to the state being used by any religious group, Catholic or Protestant, to compel, prohibit or prosecute the free exercise of any other religion. And that goes for any persecution at any time, by anyone, in any country.

And I hope that you and I condemn with equal fervor those nations which deny their Presidency to Protestants and those which deny it to Catholics. And rather than cite the misdeeds of those who differ, I would also cite the record of the Catholic Church in such nations as France and Ireland —and the independence of such statesmen as deGaulle and Adenauer.

But let me stress again that these are my views—for, contrary to common newspaper usage, I am not a Catholic candidate for President. I am the Democratic party's candidate for President who happens also to be a Catholic.

I do not speak for my church on public matters—and the church does not speak for me.

Whatever issue may come before me as President, if I should be elected—on birth control, divorce, censorship, gambling, or any other subject—I will make my decision in accordance with what my conscience tells me to be in the national interest, and without regard to outside religious pressure or dictate. And no power or threat of punishment could cause me to decide otherwise.

But if the time should ever come—and I do not concede any conflict to be remotely possible—when my office would require me to either violate my conscience, or violate the national interest, then I would resign the office, and I hope any other conscientious public servant would do likewise.

But I do not intend to apologize for these views to my critics of either Catholic or Protestant faith, nor do I intend to disavow either my views or my church in order to win this election. If I should lose on the real issues, I shall return to my seat in the Senate satisfied that I tried my best and was fairly judged.

But if this election is decided on the basis that 40,000,000 Americans lost their chance of being President on the day they were baptized, then it is the whole nation that will be the loser in the eyes of Catholics and non-catholics around the world, in the eyes of history, and in the eyes of our own people.

But if, on the other hand, I should win this election, I shall devote every effort of mind and spirit to fulfilling the oath of the Presidency—practically identical, I might add, with the oath I have taken for fourteen years in the Congress. For, without reservation, I can, and I quote, "solemnly swear that I will faithfully execute the office of President of the United States and will to the best of my ability preserve, protect and defend the Constitution, so help me God."

Questions

1. What carryovers from revivalism can you find in the present?
2. Name and locate five additional Utopian Socialist communities founded by religious groups.
3. What were the beliefs held by each of the following denominations: Unitarians, Universalists, Universal Friends, Campbell's Disciples, Shakers, Rappites, Transcendentalists, Separatists of Zoar, and Amana Society?

4. According to their "Articles of Faith," how does the creed of the Mormons differ from other religions?
5. What is the status of the Mormons in terms of membership and social and political influence in your state today?
6. What social issues outside the field of education continue to divide American society on religious lines?
7. Name non-Protestants who currently hold or recently held high political office in your city or state.

Suggested Readings

Among the numerous accounts of the wide variety of denominations that developed in the United States are:

Beardsley, Harry. *Joseph Smith and His Mormon Empire*. Boston: Houghton Mifflin Co., 1951.

Bestor, Arthur. *Backwoods Utopias*. Philadelphia: University of Pennsylvania Press, 1950.

Dunn, William. *What Happened to Religious Education? 1776–1861*. Baltimore: Johns Hopkins Press, 1958.

Hutchison, William. *The Transcendentalist Ministers: Church Reform in the New England Renaissance*. New Haven: Yale University Press, 1959.

Smith, Timothy. *Revivalism and Social Reform in Mid-nineteenth-century America*. Nashville: Abingdon Press, 1957.

Tyler, Alice Felt. *Freedom's Ferment*. Minneapolis: University of Minnesota Press, 1944.

Weisberger, Bernard. *They Gathered at the River*. New York: Little, Brown & Co., 1958.

The history of Catholicism in America is developed in:

Barrett, Patricia. *Religious Liberty and the American Presidency*. New York: Herder & Herder, 1963.

Blanchard, Paul. *American Freedom and Catholic Power*. Boston: Beacon Press, 1958.

Cogley, John. *Catholic America*. New York: Dial Press, 1973.

Cowan, Wayne, ed. *Facing Protestant-Roman Catholic Tensions*. New York: Association Press, 1960.

Maynard, Theodore. *The Story of American Catholicism*. New York: Macmillan, 1941.

Murray, John Courtney. *We Hold These Truths: Catholic Reflections on the American Proposition*. New York: Sheed & Ward, 1961.

5. New Directions

In the realm of thought majorities do not determine. Each brain is a kingdom, each mind is a sovereign. The universality of a belief does not ever tend to prove its truth.

—*Ralph Ingersoll*

Just as in earlier times, religion in the United States at the end of the 19th and beginning of the 20th centuries was affected by the social and economic changes that were transforming American life. The nation now reached from coast to coast; its population had soared as a result of natural increases and heavy immigration; countless millions of acres were brought under cultivation, scores of cities were springing up and mushrooming in size almost overnight; manufacture, the factory system, and corporate enterprise had converted the economy from an agricultural to an industrial one; and the American people themselves evolved into a complexly structured society. Once again, organized churches and religious doctrine itself were subject to challenges and had to modify themselves.

New Truths

During the second half of the 19th century the natural and social sciences underwent an explosion in new knowledge and theory. As before, the work of astronomers and geologists contradicted the biblical descriptions of the origin of the universe, the beginnings of life, and the special creation of man. In addition, the new disciplines of sociology and anthropology, along with a more critical study of biblical texts, served to support the rejection of traditional dogmas. The field that most profoundly shook traditional beliefs was biology, specifically the theory of evolution as advanced by Charles Darwin in his *Origin of Species* in 1859 and *Descent of Man* in 1871.

Darwinian evolution stirred up a controversy that raged for decades among scientists, theologians, and philosophers on both sides of the Atlantic. Almost all the churches and most of the clergy fought bitterly against the theories of natural selection and the evolvement of man from lower species of the animal kingdom. Not only did they contradict the biblical account in Genesis, but they supported the whole scientific challenge to revealed religion. Some ministers who accepted the new ideas were ousted from their pulpits or subjected to heresy trials by their church organizations.

Several state legislatures banned the teaching of evolution from the public schools.

In addition to internal doctrinal disputes among clergymen, some sweeping changes in religion occurred. One response was to establish new churches or societies. One was The Church of Christ (Scientist) established by Mary Baker Eddy. She taught that matter, disease, and sin did not exist and identified God with mind and good. Jesus had come to earth to redeem mankind from sickness and death. Her disciples, known as Christian Scientists, believe that by understanding and following these principles they can heal themselves as well as others. Another response to new scientific information was that taken by a group that rejected theology, the Society for Ethical Culture founded by Felix Adler in 1876. Still another was the total rejection of the supernatural and the denial of the existence of God. This is atheism.

Agnosticism, akin to but not the same as atheism, was another form of freethinking. It was championed by a number of public figures, journalists, and authors. The man who became most identified with it in the minds of most Americans was Colonel Robert J. Ingersoll. Ingersoll was a prominent lawyer, a leader in the Republican party and, above all, a brilliant orator. He lectured widely and wrote a number of articles on agnosticism, so that hundreds of thousands were exposed to his views. The following reading is taken from "Why Am I an Agnostic?" which appeared in *The North American Review* in December, 1889. How is Ingersoll influenced by science? Why does he reject the beliefs of the Deists and other freethinking religions? How does he explain belief in the supernatural and God? What does he find wrong with Christianity and other "national" religions? What is agnosticism?

Why Am I an Agnostic?

Robert E. Ingersoll

"With thoughts beyond the reaches of our souls."

The same rules or laws of probability must govern in religious questions as in others. There is no subject—and can be none—concerning which any human being is under any obligation to believe without evidence. Neither is there any intelligent being who can, by any possibility, be flattered by the exercise of ignorant credulity. The man who, without prejudice, reads and understands the Old and New Testaments will cease to be an orthodox Christian. The intelligent man who investigates the religion of any country without fear and without prejudice will not and cannot be a believer.

Most people, after arriving at the conclusion that Jehovah is not God, that the Bible is not an inspired book, and that the Christian religion, like other religions, is the creation of man, usually say: "There must be a Supreme Being, but Jehovah is not his name, and the Bible is not his word. There must be somewhere an overruling Providence or Power."

This position is just as untenable as the other. He who cannot harmonize the cruelties of the Bible with the goodness of Jehovah, cannot harmonize the cruelties of Nature with the goodness and wisdom of a supposed Deity. He will find it impossible to account for pestilence and famine, for earthquake and storm, for slavery, for the triumph of the strong over the weak, for the countless victories of injustice. He will find it impossible to account for martyrs—for the burning of the good, the noble, the loving, by the ignorant, the malicious, and the infamous.

How can the Deist satisfactorily account for the sufferings of women and children? In what way will he justify religious persecution—the flame and sword of religious hatred? Why did his God sit idly on his throne and allow his enemies to wet their swords in the blood of his friends? Why did he not answer the prayers of the imprisoned, of the helpless? And when he heard the lash upon the naked back of the slave, why did he not also hear the prayer of the slave? And when children were sold from the breasts of mothers, why was he deaf to the mother's cry?

It seems to me that the man who knows the limitations of the mind, who gives the proper value to human testimony, is necessarily an Agnostic. He gives up the hope of ascertaining first or final causes, of comprehending the supernatural, or of conceiving of an infinite personality. From out the words Creator, Preserver, and Providence, all meaning falls.

The mind of man pursues the path of least resistance, and the conclusions arrived at by the individual depend upon the nature and structure of his mind, on his experience, on hereditary drifts and tendencies, and on the countless things that constitute the difference in minds. One man, finding himself in the midst of mysterious phenomena, comes to the conclusion that all is the result of design; that back of all things is an infinite personality—that is to say, an infinite man; and he accounts for all that is by simply saying that the universe was created and set in motion by this infinite personality, and that it is miraculously and supernaturally governed and preserved. This man sees with perfect clearness that matter could not create itself, and therefore he imagines a creator of matter. He is perfectly satisfied that there is design in the world, and that consequently there must have been a designer. It does not occur to him that it is necessary to account for the existence of an infinite personality. He is perfectly certain that there can be no design without a designer, and he is equally certain that there can be a designer who was not designed. The absurdity becomes so great that it takes the place of a demonstration. He takes it for granted that matter was created and that its creator was not. He assumes that a creator existed from eternity without cause, and created what is called matter out of nothing; or, whereas there was nothing, this creator made the something that we call substance. . . .

Probably a very large majority of mankind believe in the existence of supernatural beings, and a majority of what are known as the civilized nations, in an infinite personality. In the realm of thought majorities do not determine. Each brain is a kingdom, each mind is a sovereign.

The universality of a belief does not even tend to prove its truth. A large majority of mankind have believed in what is known as God, and an equally large majority have as implicitly believed in what is known as the Devil. These beings have been inferred from phenomena. They were produced for the most part by ignorance, by fear, and by selfishness. Man in all ages has endeavored to account for the mysteries of life and death, of substance, of force, for the ebb and flow of things, for earth and star. The savage, dwelling in his cave, subsisting on roots and reptiles, or on beasts that could be slain with club and stone, surrounded by countless objects of terror, standing by rivers, so far as he knew, without source or end, by seas with but one shore, the prey of beasts mightier than himself, of diseases strange and fierce, trembling at the voice of thunder, blinded by the lightning, feeling the earth shake beneath him, seeing the sky lurid with the volcano's glare,—fell prostrate and begged for the protection of the Unknown.

In the long night of savagery, in the midst of pestilence and famine, through the long and dreary winters, crouched in dens of darkness, the seeds of superstition were sown in the brain of man. The savage believed, and thoroughly believed, that everything happened in reference to him; that he by his actions could excite the anger, or by his worship placate the wrath, of the Unseen. He resorted to flattery and prayer. To the best of his ability he put in stone, or rudely carved in wood, his idea of this god. For this idol he built a hut, a hovel, and at last a cathedral. Before these images he bowed, and at these shrines, whereon he lavished his wealth, he sought protection for himself and for the ones he loved. The few took advantage of the ignorant many. They pretended to have received messages from the Unknown. They stood between the helpless multitude and the gods. They were the carriers of flags of truce. At the court of heaven they presented the cause of man, and upon the labor of the deceived they lived.

The Christian of to-day wonders at the savage who bowed before his idol; and yet it must be confessed that the god of stone answered prayer and protected his worshippers precisely as the Christian's God answers prayer and protects his worshippers to-day. . . .

Heredity is on the side of superstition. All our ignorance pleads for the old. In most men there is a feeling that their ancestors were exceedingly good and brave and wise, and that in all things pertaining to religion their conclusions should be followed. They believe that their fathers and mothers were of the best, and that that which satisfied them should satisfy their children. With a feeling of reverence they say that the religion of their mother is good enough and pure enough and reasonable enough, for them. In this way the love of parents and the reverence for ancestors have unconsciously bribed the reason and put out, or rendered exceedingly dim, the eyes of the mind.

There is a kind of longing in the heart of the old to live and die where their parents lived and died—a tendency to go back to the homes of their youth. Around the old oak of manhood grow and cling these vines. Yet it will hardly do to say that the religion of my mother is good enough for me, any more than to say the geology, or the astronomy, or the philosophy of my mother is good enough for me. Every human being is entitled to the best he can obtain; and if there has been the slightest improvement on the religion of the mother, the son is entitled to that improvement, and he should not deprive himself of that advantage by the mistaken idea that he owes it to his mother to perpetuate, in a reverential way, her ignorant mistakes.

If we are to follow the religion of our fathers and mothers, our fathers and mothers should have followed the religion of theirs. Had this been done, there could have been no improvement in the world of thought. The first religion would have been the last, and the child would have died as ignorant as the mother. Progress would have been impossible, and on the graves of ancestors would have been sacrificed the intelligence of mankind. . . .

The average man adopts the religion of his country, or, rather, the religion of his country adopts him. He is dominated by the egotism of race, the arrogance of nation, and the prejudice called patriotism. He does not reason—he feels. He does not investigate—he believes. To him the religions of other nations are absurd and infamous, and their gods monsters of ignorance and cruelty. In every country this average man is taught, first, that there is a supreme being; second, that he has made known his will; third, that he will reward the true believer; fourth, that he will punish the unbeliever, the scoffer, and the blasphemer; fifth, that certain ceremonies are pleasing to this god; sixth, that he has established a church; and seventh, that priests are his representatives on earth. And the average man has no difficulty in determining that the god of his nation is the true God; that the will of this true God is contained in the sacred scriptures of his nation; that he is one of the true believers, and that the people of other nations—that is, believing other religions—are scoffers; that the only true church is the one to which he belongs; and that the priests of his country are the only ones who have had or ever will have the slightest influence with this true God. All these absurdities to the average man seem self-evident propositions; and so he holds all other creeds in scorn, and congratulates himself that he is a favorite of the one true God.

If the average Christian had been born in Turkey, he would have been a Mohammedan; and if the average Mohammedan had been born in New England and educated at Andover, he would have regarded the damnation of the heathen as the "tidings of great joy." . . .

Has a man the right to examine, to investigate, the religion of his own country—the religion of his father and mother? Christians admit that the citizens of all countries not Christian have not only this right, but that it is their solemn duty. Thousands of missionaries are sent to heathen countries to persuade the believers of other religions not only to examine their superstitions, but to renounce them, and to adopt those of the missionaries. It is the duty of a heathen to disregard the religion of his country and to hold in contempt the creed of his father and of his mother. If the citizens of heathen nations have the right to examine the foundations of their religion, it would seem that the citizens of Christian nations have the same right. Christians, however, go further than this; they say to the heathen: You must examine your religion, and not only so, but you must reject it; and, unless you do reject it, and, in addition to such rejection, adopt ours, you will be eternally damned. Then these same Christians say to the inhabitants of a Christian country: You must not examine; you must not investigate; but whether you examine or not, you must believe, or you will be eternally damned.

If there be one true religion, how is it possible to ascertain which of all the religions the true one is? There is but one way. We must impartially examine the claims of all. The right to examine involves the necessity to accept or reject. Understand me, not the right to accept or reject, but the necessity. From this conclusion there is no possible escape. If, then, we have the right to examine, we have the right to tell the conclusion reached. Christians have examined other religions somewhat, and they have expressed their opinion with the utmost freedom—that is to say, they have denounced them all as false and fraudulent; have called their gods idols and myths, and their priests impostors.

The Christian does not deem it worth while to read the Koran. Probably not one Christian in a thousand ever saw a copy of that book. And yet all Christians are perfectly satisfied that the Koran is the work of an impostor. No Presbyterian thinks it is worth his while to examine the religious systems of India; he knows that the Brahmins are mistaken, and that all their miracles are falsehoods. No Methodist cares to read the life of Buddha, and no Baptist will waste his time studying the ethics of Confucius. Christians of every sort and kind take it for granted that there is only one true religion, and that all except Christianity are absolutely without foundation. The Christian world believes that all the prayers of India are unanswered; that all the sacrifices upon the countless altars of Egypt, of Greece, and of Rome were without effect. They believe that all these mighty nations worshipped their gods in vain; that their priests were deceivers or deceived; that their ceremonies were wicked or meaningless; that their temples were built by ignorance and fraud and that no God heard their songs of praise, their cries of despair, their words of thankfulness; that on account of their religion no pestilence was stayed; that the earthquake and volcano, the flood and storm went on their ways of death—while the real God looked on and laughed at their calamities and mocked at their fears.

We find now that the prosperity of nations has depended, not upon their religion, not upon the goodness or providence of some god, but on soil and climate and commerce, upon the ingenuity, industry and courage of the people, upon the development of the mind, on the spread of education, on the liberty of thought and action; and that in this mighty panorama of national life, reason has built and superstition has destroyed.

Being satisfied that all believe precisely as they must, and that religions have been naturally produced, I have neither praise nor blame for any man. Good men have had bad creeds, and bad men have had good ones. Some of the noblest of the human race have fought and died for the wrong. The brain of man has been the trysting-place of contradictions. Passion often masters reason. . . .

In the discussion of theological or religious questions, we have almost passed the personal phase, and we are now weighing arguments instead of exchanging epithets and curses. They who really seek for truth must be the best of friends. Each knows that his desire can never take the place of fact, and that, next to finding truth, the greatest honor must be won in honest search.

We see that many ships are driven in many ways by the same wind. So men, reading the same book, write many creeds and lay out many roads to heaven. To the best of my ability, I have examined the religions of many countries and the creeds of many sects. They are much alike, and the testimony by which they are substantiated is of such a character that to those who believe is promised an eternal reward. In all the sacred books there are some truths, some rays of light, some words of love and hope. The face of savagery is sometimes softened by a smile—the human triumphs, and the heart breaks into song. But in these books are also found the words of fear and hate, and from their pages crawl serpents that coil and hiss in all the paths of men.

For my part, I prefer the books that inspiration has not claimed. Such is the nature of my brain that Shakespeare gives me greater joy than all the prophets of the ancient world. There are thoughts that satisfy the hunger of the mind. I am convinced that Humboldt knew more of geology than the author of Genesis; that Darwin was a greater naturalist than he who told the story of the flood; that Laplace was better acquainted with the habits of the sun and moon than Joshua could have been, and that Haeckel, Huxley, and Tyndall know more about the earth and stars, about the history of man, the philosophy of life—more that is of use, ten thousand times—than all the writers of the sacred books.

I believe in the religion of reason—the gospel of this world; in the development of the mind, in the accumulation of intellectual wealth, to the end that man may free himself from superstitious fear, to the end that he may take advantage of the forces of nature to feed and clothe the world.

Let us be honest with ourselves. In the presence of countless mysteries; standing beneath the boundless heaven sown thick with constellations; knowing that each grain of sand, each leaf, each blade of grass, asks of every mind the answerless question; knowing that the simplest thing defies solution; feeling that we deal with the superficial and the relative, and that we are forever eluded by the real, the absolute,—let us admit the limitations of our minds, and let us have the courage and the candor to say: We do not know.

* * *

New Purposes

The post-Civil War transformation of society brought on by urbanization and industrialization had important consequences for organized religion. Churches could not long remain oblivious to the increasingly serious problems of slums, poverty, broken homes, alcoholism, single young men and young women living in cities without family influence, sweat shops, low wages, and unemployment. As had happened in England, there sprang up in American cities such institutions as the Young Men's Christian Association, the Young Women's Christian Association, the Salvation Army, Goodwill Industries, and settlement houses such as the pioneer Hull House in Chicago. Emulating a long-established practice among Catholic churches of providing a broad variety of social and charitable services to their parishioners, certain Protestant ones, forced to contend with a loss of membership in working-class neighborhoods and the growing incidence of crime, prostitution, and social dysfunction, began to operate on a seven-day-a-week basis and reach out into the community. These institutional churches added lecture halls, classrooms, libraries and gymnasiums, established adult education and vocational training programs, and became hosts to such organizations as the Scouts, nurseries, men's and women's clubs, and athletic associations.

Some ministers, however, felt that these social programs, worthy as they were, dealt only with symptoms but did not get to the root of the problem. They were convinced that all the human misery they saw around them was evidence that there was something wrong with society and the economic system operating in the country, and they considered it their Christian duty to do something about it. They felt that churches had lost touch with the downtrodden masses of people and had become the allies, if not the tools, of the rich and the business community. From these attitudes, the Social Gospel movement began among certain Protestant churches. Started in the 1880s, it continued to World War I. It had its counterpart in Catholic cir-

cles as a result of the progressive encyclical *Rerum Novarum* issued by Pope
Leo XIII in 1891.

The Social Gospel movement went through two phases. The first,
known as Social Christianity, was a more moderate, reformist one designed
to alleviate the conditions of the poor. The other, more "radical" one, Christian Socialism, attacked the existing order. A leading exponent of the first
was Washington Gladden, a Congregational minister in Columbus, Ohio.
The following reading is taken from his book, *Applied Christianity*, published in 1886. What does he find wrong with the nation's economic system?
On what does he base his views on religion? What reforms does he recommend? Why is it proper to classify him as a moderate?

Applied Christianity

Washington Gladden

But now comes a harder question. How is this growing wealth divided?
Is it rightly or wrongly divided? If it is wrongly divided, has the Christian
moralist anything to say about a better way? Christianity, as we have seen,
has much to do with the production of wealth; has it anything to do with its
distribution? . . .

Plainly there is something out of joint in our machinery of distribution,
or this state of things could not be. During the past fourteen years the
wealth of this nation has increased much faster than the population, but the
people who work for wages are little if any better off than they were fourteen years ago. It is doubtful whether the average yearly wages of the mechanic, the laborer, or the operative will purchase for him more of the necessaries of life now than at that time. At any rate, the gain, if gain there has
been, must be very slight. What is true of the wage-laborer is true, also, of
the small trader who subsists upon the laborer's patronage, and also quite
largely of clerks and of teachers, as well as of those professional men whose
services are chiefly in request among the poorer classes. There is a considerable class in the community whose fortunes are closely linked with those of
the wage-laborers.

This, then, is the existing state of things. The production of wealth in
the country increases enormously year by year; the workingman's share of
what is produced, and the share of those economically affiliated with the
workingman, increases very slowly. . . .

What has the Christian moralist to say about this state of things? He is
bound to say that it is a bad state of things, and must somehow be reformed.
He is bound to declare that "the laborer is worthy of his hire"; that, in the
words of the apostle Paul, "the husbandman that laboreth must be the first
to partake of the fruits." The broad equities of Christ's rule demand that

this great increase of wealth be made, somehow, to inure to the benefit, in a far larger degree, of the people by whose labor it is produced. He will not deny that the capitalist should have a fair reward for his prudence and his abstinence; he will not refuse to the "undertaker," the *entrepreneur,* the organizer of labor, who stands between capitalist and laborer, enabling them to combine in the production of wealth, that large reward to which his superior intelligence and experience entitle him; but he will still insist that the workman ought to have a larger share. . . . And Christianity, by the lips of all its teachers, ought with all its emphasis to say to society: "Your present industrial system, which fosters these enormous inequalities, which permits a few to heap up most of the gains of this advancing civilization, and leaves the many without any substantial share in them, is an inadequate and inequitable system, and needs important changes to make it the instrument of righteousness."

But when this testimony is borne, we shall hear men answering after this fashion: "Suppose it is wrong; what are you going to do about it? Would you have the state take possession of all the property and divide it equally among its citizens?" . . .

First, then, it is undoubtedly the duty of Christians to do what they can by means of law to secure a better industrial system. But this is not saying that Christians should ask the state to take the property of the rich and distribute it among the poor. It is true that the state does something in that direction already. It takes, by taxation, the property of the rich in large amounts, and expends it for the benefit of all, the poor equally with the rich. Thousands who pay no taxes at all have the full benefit of streets, street-lamps, sewers, side-walks, water, police, fire department, and schools, not to speak of important provisions made exclusively for the poor, such as city physicians and dispensaries, alms-houses, insane hospitals, and the like. The destitute classes thus get the benefit of a considerable distribution of property annually enforced by the state. And it is pretty clear that the state is now going quite as far in this direction as it is safe to go. Certainly we want no more eleemosynary distribution of money by the state than we have now. The time may come when the nation will be compelled to take under its control, if not into its ownership, the railroads and the telegraphs, and administer them for the common good. They are falling, in far too large a degree, into the hands of men who use them for the spoiling of our commerce and the corruption of our politics. But the wisdom or the equity of this measure is not yet so clear that it can be demanded as an act of public justice, and therefore the Christian moralist will not yet venture to pronounce upon it.

There are, however, one or two things that he will insist upon as the immediate duty of the state. Certain outrageous monopolies exist that the state is bound to crush. It is an outrage on public justice that half a dozen men should be able to control the entire fuel supply of New York and New

England, forbidding the miners to work more than two or three days in a week, lest the operatives of the New England mills or the longshoremen of the New York wharves should get their coal at a little smaller price per ton. The forcible suppression of an industry by which one of the necessaries of life is furnished, this violent interference with the natural laws of trade in the interest of a few monopolists, is so contrary to public justice and public policy that some way must be found of making an end of it. The coal barons must not be permitted to enrich themselves by compelling the miners to starve at one end of their lines and the operatives to freeze at the other. In like manner the great lines of transportation from the West are under the control of three or four men, and although they have not hitherto been able to combine in such a way as greatly to enhance the price of breadstuffs, it is not improbable that combinations will yet take place by which such a levy will be made upon the food of the nation. Even now the oil in the poor man's lamp is heavily taxed by a greedy monopoly. All these iniquitous encroachments upon the rights of the people must be arrested; and it is the duty of every Christian, as the servant of a God of justice and righteousness, to say so in terms that cannot be misunderstood.

Another gigantic public evil that the state must exterminate is that of gambling in stocks and produce. This system of gambling in margins is a system of piracy; by means of it hundreds of millions of dollars are plundered every year from the industrial classes. It is treason to say that it cannot be put down; it must be put down or it will destroy the nation. It is the vampire that is sucking the life-blood of our commerce; it is the dragon that is devouring the moral vigor of our young men. When these monsters of the Stock and Produce Exchanges are killed, and a few of our great monopolies are laid low, the greatest obstructions to a free distribution of wealth will be removed, and the working classes will secure a larger share of the product of their industry than they are getting now. All such violent hindrances to a free and fair exchange of commodities and services—all such hungry parasites of industry—the state is bound to remove, and Christian morality calls on all its professors to enforce this obligation on the state. . . .

All that intelligent Christians will ask the state to do, therefore, toward promoting the distribution of wealth, is to provide for the general welfare, as it now does, by taxation; to protect all classes in the exercise of their rights; to strike down those foes that now clutch our industries by the throat, and then to leave the natural laws of trade and the motives of humanity and good-will to effect a more equitable distribution.

*   *   *

The more militant clergymen were not content to have the country continue to operate within the existing socioeconomic order. They felt that free-enterprise capitalism itself was the root of society's ills and was anti-thetical to the fundamental principles of Christianity. They asserted that piecemeal reform was not enough and turned to socialism. Rejecting the materialism and antireligious bias of the Marxists, they found their proper direction in cooperation and communal sharing.

One outstanding spokesman of Christian Socialism was George V. Herron, a Congregational minister who taught at Grinnell College, Iowa. The following selection is taken from his book, *The New Redemption,* published in 1893. What things does Herron see wrong with the nation's economic and social life and to what does he attribute them? What does he mean when he advocates that the state follow the Sermon on the Mount and the social constitution of Jesus? In what ways does he find Christian principles being violated? Although he recommends no concrete changes, what does he call for?

The New Redemption
George V. Herron

It is hardly disputed that capital, under our modern industrial system, is receiving more than a just share of the fruits of labor, and the laborer is receiving relatively less and less of the profits of his toil. The increase of wealth and wages is in no sense equitable. There is not a progressive econo-mist in America or England who does not say that wealth is growing out of all proportion to the benefits that the laborer derives from his labor. The distribution of wealth is not according to industry or ability; not according to one's worth in society; but according in large measure to the skill of some in appropriating to themselves the fruits of the labor of others by commercial legerdemain. It is thus that while we are the richest nation on the globe our wealth is rapidly being centered in the hands of a few and industrial toilers are being reduced to a condition of practical servitude. "Thoughtful men see and admit," says Judge Walter Q. Gresham, "that our country is becoming less and less democratic and more and more plutocratic," and plutocracy he pronounces the most insidious of all forms of tyranny. "Nothing," says Dr. Theodore Dwight Woolsey, "would lead the mass of men to embrace social-ism sooner than the conviction that this enormous accumulation of capital in a few hands was to be not only an evil in fact, if not prevented, but a necessary evil beyond prevention. . . . A revolution, slow or rapid, would certainly bring about a new order of things." Nor can the difference between the work-ing and capitalistic classes be concealed by the fact that wages average better than forty or fifty years ago. It is a waste of time to cite statistics to show that the laboring man has economic goods he did not formerly have. Forty to fifty years ago the mechanic and his master worked side by side; the apprentice was the social equal of his employer. There was not the stratification of society which we now see, and almost every man produced something of his own livelihood. Fuel cost him but the work of bringing it to his door yard. He raised necessities which must now be purchased. The lowest wages of a half a century ago represented a more equitable share in the *social* benefits of civilization than the highest wages of to-day. And the inevitable result of the system of wages and competition will be to increase social inequalities, to increase the wealth of a few and the poverty of the many. It is to the interest of capital, when it releases itself from moral and social obligations, and looks only to its own increase, to keep a huge class of unemployed men, who must work or starve. The present industrial system could not exist were it not for the fact that great multitudes of the unemployed have been brought to this country, systematically and purposely, for the sake of reducing wages and producing a state of poverty. By this method the clothing trade of the United States thrives upon the sweating system. By pitting the unemployed against the employed, by reducing men and women and children to a condition of poverty, where they must work at any price or starve, competition has prospered by the blood of men and women. In the midst of great wealth, with the glory of its material enterprise, its blind luxury and mad speculation, its disregard for human life, for moral law, there is an increasing poverty and degradation; a deep and angry social discontent; a growing distrust in the reality of our liberties and the sincerity of our Christianity, proving that our competitive system does not belong to a divine order of things. It is unnatural that the strong should prosper at the expense of the weak; that the earning of one's daily bread should be an uncertain strife. It is a violation of nature that prosperity should come through the triumph of cunning over character, and the conflict of selfish interests. Our so-called industrial order is the disordering of nature. It is the disorganization of human life. There is enough in this world for all to have and enjoy in abundance, if there were a system by which there could be an equitable distribution of that abundance upon the principles of the divine economy.

The social problem is the call of the state to become Christian. The state can save itself only by believing in the Lord Jesus Christ as the supreme authority in law, politics, and society. The state is the social organ. To meet the strain that will be put upon it by the revolution, *the state must be redeemed from the worship of property and from commercial theories of government*. It can prove its right to be only by procuring a greater measure of social justice and giving a larger recognition to the sacredness of man. The state must have in it the mind that was in Jesus, who is the final political economist. The Sermon on the Mount is the science of society, it is a treatise on political economy; it is a system of justice. It consists of the natural laws which proceed from the heart of God, and operate in the creation and redemption of the world; in the evolution of man and the progressive development of society. It is the constitution of the divine and universal society which John in the Revelation calls a new earth. The establishment of its justice underneath the politics and social structures of man is the new Jerusalem which John saw coming down out of heaven from God. The business of the state is to adopt this social constitution of Jesus as the spirit and justice of the people, and bring every activity into subjection to its authority. It is not primarily the mission of the state to protect property as a thing in itself. *The state is the organization of the life of man in unity with the life of God; its concern is with human beings.* Property is valuable only as it is the instrument of justice between man and man, and a bond of fellowship with God. Property has a right to protection only as it is designedly working out the whole welfare of man. It is the business of the state to develop and shield the common manhood and happiness, the physical and moral health, of men as sons of God. Government has a right to existence and authority for no other end than that for which God sent his only begotten Son into the world. It is the vocation of the state, as the social organ, to so control property, so administer the production and distribution of economic goods, as to give to every man the fruit of his labor, and protect the laborer from the irresponsible tyranny of the passion for wealth. It is the duty of the state to so reconstruct itself as to procure for every man full opportunity to develop all his powers, and to see that no member of society suffers for the want of work and bread.

A baseless assumption which the state must correct is, that employers have an economic right to employ and discharge from the individual standpoint, with only a money obligation to employees, and no responsibility to society. But the Christian state, as the organization of the divine life of man, is bound to deny the existence of any such right in a moral world. The assertion of such a right is the denial of the humanity of man; it is infidelity to Christ: it is substantial atheism. The assumption that capital may discharge and employ solely on the basis of self-interest shuts God out of human affairs and denies the brotherhood of man. It is social anarchism. It is the declaration on the part of capital that it will not submit to law. He who sets himself apart from social relationships, to do what he pleases with his own, upon the ground of pure individualism, asserts the right to do what God himself dare not do. In so far as the state allows the assumption and exercise of such a right, it fails to secure justice. No industrial concern has a right to receive the benefits of society without bearing commensurate responsibilities. It is monstrous and undemocratic, it is the enthronement of industrial despotism, for the state to grant powers and protection to corporate or individual employers, and yet leave them irresponsible for the social welfare. The assertion on the part of capital of a right to exist for the sake of gain, independent of the voice of the people or the welfare of labor, has had its day. It is the last remnant of that absolutism which has been slowly and revengefully yielding to the redemptive forces that have been making men free ever since the Son of man poured out his life upon the Calvary of truth. There was a day when men thought the state could be preserved only by maintaining the absolute authority of the king, and by giving the people no voice in their government. Men once believed that the divine right of kings alone could secure political order and procure social justice. But that day has gone by, and democracy every where has the political field, or is gaining it in every civilized nation. *Absolutism of every sort is doomed and cannot hold its own against the purposes of God. It can no more sustain itself in industry than in politics. If democracy is good for the state, it is good for industry.* King George's assertion of a right to tax American colonists without representation, was not half as unjust, as intolerable and despotic, as the assumption that a great corporation can enjoy the nurture and claim the protection of society, and yet deny society all management or voice in its affairs. A man could not have what he calls his own, save through the co-operation of his fellow-men; and they have rights in the management of capital for the social welfare commensurate with the privileges and opportunities which capital receives. If democracy, which is social fellowship and political mutualism, can best procure political justice and preserve the state, then it can also procure the largest economic justice and industrial freedom. Capital is a social creation, and its administration a social responsibility; so that industrial federation lies in the nature of things.

But the initiative in the establishment of a democracy of Jesus in the world of work and wealth must be taken by capital itself, which has in its hands both the power and the responsibility. The commercial dogma that capital has discharged its duty when it has paid its employees the market rate of wages, with the market under the sovereignty of what is known as the law of supply and demand, asserts the supremacy of capital over moral law, and gives to it a worth greater than the worth of human life. *Labor is not a commodity any more than human souls are a commodity; labor is life.* The relation between employer and employee is a sacred relationship; a relationship that must not be sundered by mere caprice or self-interest. It is the utter disregard of the sacredness of this relationship by both employer and employee, treating it as simply a money relationship, that is the root of the strife between the two. The union of men in industry is a communion of human lives for divine ends; and the selfish severing of this union is not merely a violation of the Sermon on the Mount; it is economic foolishness and social lawlessness. Capital should recognize that the life of the laborer is a greater matter than the gain of the employer. It was Lincoln's belief that labor should own capital, in opposition to the slave-owner's view that capital should own labor. The history of industry bears out the belief that wherever there has been a recognition of the manhood of labor on the part of capital, with the spirit of social fellowship and Christian democracy, there have been peace and prosperity for both employer and workman. The love that moved

God to give his only begotten Son to save the world must be the law that shall govern wealth, and move its possessors to consecrate themselves to the creation of a Christian society and Christian state. It lies within the power of the American capitalists who call themselves Christian, by taking the Sermon on the Mount and patiently working it into the foundations of industry, to be the creators of a new and divine civilization that would surpass all our apprehensions of the Revelation of John. If they would take the Sermon on the Mount as economic law, as a revelation of the nature of things, as the safest basis upon which the market of the world could stand, they would lift the commerce and industry of the world above the chance and strife of competing interests, and make the moving trains of merchandise, the toil of the mills and echo of the mines, the barter and exchange of the markets, all accordant parts of a harmony of divine justice. *I do not believe there can ever be peace between man and man, between interest and interest, between class and class, by any other mode than through the belief of capital, the belief of industry, the belief of the market, in the naturalness, in the wisdom, in the safety, of the moral law of Jesus. This the church must teach, and its members must cease to promulgate social atheism. It cannot be stated too plainly that either the people will become atheistic, or the wealth which is in Christian hands must obey the social laws of the Sermon on the Mount.* Either its laws are practicable, reasonable, and natural, and will give the largest prosperity to all, or men will not believe in an all-good and all-wise God. Obedience to Christ's laws would give a new redemption to man that would be the creation of a new earth, overspread with the healing wisdom of a new heaven of divine truth, from which the sea of social troubles would flee away forever. . . .

It is to-day the one emergent mission of the church to bring together in a divine unity the various human interests that are now at strife. The whole conception of the necessary antagonism between capital and labor is not simply an economic and political falsehood, not only a peril to the state and a denial of justice, but it makes Christianity an ideal impossible of realization. The church must demand social conditions that shall realize the Christian gospel. Unto it has been given the message that the interest of one man is the interest of all. The interest of labor is the interest of capital; and the interest of capital is the interest of labor. When capital keeps from labor its Christian share of the produce of labor, it injures itself; and labor injures itself in destroying capital. The church must open the eyes of men to see the wisdom and power of living for the common good, to the practical atheism and anarchism of selfish principles, and declare love to be the natural law of industrial activity and social life. Love at the heart of society, love at the heart of the state, love in the heart of the church, love at the heart of commerce, will right our economic wrongs, give labor its just rewards, and diffuse among the people the benefits of civilization. Only by obedience to the law of love can society be regenerated and historic problems be solved.

There is in love alone the power to dispel the clouds of darkness that now over-gloom the earth with peril and judgment, calling for a new earth to rise to meet the descending heavens of larger truth. And the law of love can be obeyed only through communion with God and sacrifice for man.

*   *   *

The beliefs and efforts of these clergymen who advocated the Social Gospel did not go uncriticized and unchallenged, especially the more radical ones that involved a change in the socioeconomic order. Big businessmen and their supporters in university, press, and pulpit leaped to the defense of free-enterprise capitalism and the gospel of wealth. The reformation of society clashed too sharply with traditional American Protestantism, particularly its Calvinist-Puritan strain. Individual salvation was related to earthly life, at the same time that the work ethic was extolled. Those who achieved wealth through hard work, energetic drive, thrift, and prudent risk deserved it; likewise, those who were unemployed or poverty-stricken had only themselves to blame. Any tampering with the nation's economy would be a violation of natural law. This opposition prevented the Social Gospel movement from catching on more effectively. Most ministers shied away from it, and most of those who supported it only advocated its more moderate recommendations. Nevertheless, its ideals did help to reinforce the efforts of secular crusaders of the time and bring about the reforms of the Progressive Era of the early 20th century.

Questions

1. To what extent do religious leaders and natural scientists find themselves in conflict at present?
2. What is the position of your religion on Darwinian evolution?
3. Like Ingersoll, William James, the founder of the philosophy of pragmatism, was strongly influenced by science, but he rejected agnosticism. Read his *The Will to Believe* and determine why he believes in God.
4. Distinguish between deism, agnosticism, and atheism.
5. Historically speaking was the Social Gospel movement a success or a failure? Why?
6. Do you feel that the purpose and spirit behind the Social Gospel movement are stronger or weaker in organized religion today? Why?

Suggested Readings

The impact of science upon religion is examined in:

Commager, Henry Steele. *The American Mind*. New Haven: Yale University Press, 1950.

Foster, Frank. *The Modern Movement in American Theology*. New York: Revell Press, 1939.

Hofstadter, Richard. *Social Darwinism in American Thought*. Boston: Beacon Press, 1955.

Meyers, Gustavus. *History of Bigotry in the United States*. New York: Random House, 1960.

Persons, Stow, ed. *Evolutionary Thought in America*. New Haven: Yale University Press, 1950.

Raab, Earl, ed. *Religious Conflict in America*. Garden City, N.Y.: Doubleday & Co., 1964.

Warren, Sidney. *American Freethought, 1860–1914*. New York: Columbia University Press, 1943.

Weisenberger, Francis. *Ordeal of Faith*. New York: Philosophical Library, 1959.

The Social Gospel movement is dealt with in:

Dombrowski, James. *The Early Days of Christian Socialism in America*. New York: Columbia University Press, 1936.

Greene, Evarts. *Religion and the State in America*. New York: New York University Press, 1941.

Hopkins, Charles. *The Rise of the Social Gospel in American Protestantism*. New Haven: Yale University Press, 1940.

May, Henry. *Protestant Churches and Industrial America*. New York: Harper & Brothers, 1949.

Troeltsch, Ernst. *The Social Teaching of the Christian Churches*. New York: Macmillan, 1931.

6. Fixed Constitutional Star

No official yet born on this earth is wise enough or generous enough to separate good ideas from bad ideas, good beliefs from bad beliefs.

—Walter Lippmann

Because the freedom to think and believe what one wishes is the most important of all liberties, religious freedom holds a preferred position in our constitutional system. Some go so far as to assert that it is an absolute, irreducible, irrevocable right. To them the free-exercise and establishment clauses mean just what they say and should be taken literally. Their controlling element—"Congress shall make no law"—means Congress shall make *no* law. Others maintain that the issues and questions involved are complex and often conflicting. The religious liberty of any one individual must be balanced against other freedoms, against the needs of society, and against the religious liberty of other individuals. Furthermore, there are situations where the free exercise and establishment clauses need to be harmonized one with the other.

This difference in philosophy and outlook is not restricted to theoretical debate between professors of jurisprudence or constitutional lawyers; it enters into the arena of daily social relations. Controversies have raged for decades, numerous court decisions have defined and further refined the issues, and reactions to these decisions have been emotional and prolonged. Through it all, government has had to walk the tightrope of neutrality and fairness, any misstep setting off further conflict. In the words of a student of church-state relations:

> There are few things about which men disagree with such fervor and intensity as their religious beliefs. On these disagreements and differences the state must have nothing to say. No one can be free to answer for himself the important and pregnant questions of human life and destiny if any agency of the government can decide for him what rituals to practice, what ceremonies to observe, and what creeds to profess. Americans of intellect and good will—and of all faiths—have decided that their government should not use its awesome powers to support one religion in preference to others, all religions in preference to none, and none in preference to some. The Government of the United States, in harmony with its Con-

stitution, must forever maintain a neutral stance, protecting the free exercise of religion wherever it appears, and prohibiting its establishment whenever it threatens. Only in this way can every citizen practice his religion in isolation or in concert as he desires, without fear that his government will intervene. Only in this way can he be assured that the same rights of religious freedom that are guaranteed to him are guaranteed also to those who disagree with him. It is this precious right of the individual, in an area that affects the very source and destiny of his being, to which the First Amendment to the Constitution is dedicated.°

Closely related but not identical to the issue of freedom of religious conduct is the question of whether religious liberty extends to the right to teach that there is a moral obligation to disobey an existing law. It is maintained that allowing advocacy of a change in law but prohibiting advocacy of disobedience is not enough. This viewpoint holds that no limits should be placed on advocacy of disobedience on religious grounds, for communicating these ideas does not involve force since the recommendation can be heeded or ignored, and the law being opposed may deserve to be changed or eliminated. If an individual believes that a condition of society goes against the will of God and is willing to accept the penalty for disobedience, he deserves to be heard. Therefore, the principles of liberty require that advocating unlawfulness be permitted even though we prohibit unlawfulness itself. Although this makes law enforcement more difficult, according to those who hold this view it is the price that must be paid for a liberal society.

Belief and Expression

In the main, the free exercise of religion has not been a major problem or, with a few specific exceptions, a source of serious controversy since the adoption of the Constitution and the Bill of Rights. This is particularly true of those aspects of religious liberty that deal with thought, belief, expression, and certain forms of ritual. For these are also protected by the free-speech guarantee of the First Amendment. Difficulty arises when they lead to certain forms of action which transgress the law or prohibit conduct required by the state. The constitutional question immediately rises as to whether religious belief is a valid defense against violating the law. There is no responsible support for a blanket immunity from criminal prosecution because of religious conscience. As an extreme example, ritual murder can never be condoned. There are some people, however, who maintain the exact opposite position: there are no circumstances where religion can be used to justify an illegal act. To allow otherwise, they hold, would mean that the state

---

° Robert Bierstedt, "Religion, the State, the Individual," Alan Reitman, ed. *The Price of Liberty*. New York: Norton, 1968, pp. 98–99.

would be making a special dispensation for those with certain kinds of religious beliefs, an encroachment upon separation of church and state. A compromise position is held by those who assert that there are situations where certain practices should be condoned even though they are punishable as criminal acts. They contend that if the particular need of the state is weak and is clearly outweighted by the spiritual need of the individuals involved, the latter should prevail.

A concrete illustration of this can be found in a 1954 California Supreme Court decision in a case involving the use of peyote or mescaline for religious purposes by certain American Indians. The court found that the drug was an essential element in the religious observances of the Native American Church and that, although the state could establish general laws prohibiting the use of narcotics, it had no "compelling interest" in punishing the Indians for their religious ceremony.

Religious freedom in the United States differs from that of other countries because it is considered more an individual attribute or right rather than something one possesses as a member of a religious group. Hence the emphasis upon the right of *individual* conscience. So entrenched is the principle of freedom of individual belief that no cases have occurred involving efforts either to mandate or to prohibit a set of beliefs. However, several important controversies have been engendered by the attempts of government to force individuals to go against their beliefs.

An instance of this involved the constitutionality of parochial schools. In 1922, Oregon adopted a law eliminating private schools in the state and requiring that all children of school age attend only public schools. This was unanimously struck down by the Supreme Court three years later in *Pierce v. Society of Sisters*. The Court held that the requirement interfered "with the liberty of parents" in the upbringing and education of their children. Since parents of certain faiths believed it essential that their children receive a religious education, the law violated their religious liberty. A more recent instance involved an action by a state which the Constitution denied to the federal government—a religious test for office. In *Torcaso v. Watkins* (1961), the Court unanimously ruled against Maryland's requirement that an applicant for the position of notary public affirm his belief in God. It held that a religious test for office in any form violated freedom of religious belief.

But what of a religious test for office imposed not by government but by the American people themselves? The First Amendment and the rest of the Constitution do not provide any protection here. It is a matter of attitude and practice or of public opinion. The following selection raises an important question. Did the election of the first Catholic president establish that the American people had freed themselves from religious prejudice in public life, or do they have a way to go yet? The reading is from an article written by Robert Bendiner entitled "Our Right Not to Believe" which ap-

peared in *The Saturday Evening Post,* February 10, 1962. Author and jour-
nalist, Bendiner serves on the editorial board of the *New York Times.* What
official and unofficial limitations upon individual religious liberty persist in
this country? On what grounds does Bendiner find them objectionable? Why
does he review the religious attitudes of the Founding Fathers and of outstanding Americans of later times? How do you account for present-day
public opinion about the religion of elected officials?

Our Right Not to Believe
Robert Bendiner

Future historians will probably record the Presidential election of 1960
as a triumph of fairmindedness over a prejudice as old as the Republic.
They will be right, of course. And it is all the more ironic that this very
campaign, which produced our first Roman Catholic President, witnessed an
attempt to ostracize another group of Americans, entitled as much as anyone else to be judged by their public lives rather than their private beliefs.
"There is only one way that I can visualize religion being a legitimate issue
in an American political campaign," Richard Nixon said, in what was no
doubt intended as a gesture of generosity. "That would be if one of the can-
didates for the Presidency had *no* religious belief."

Politics being what it is, no one thought it surprising that Mr. Nixon's
opponent failed to make much of this cavalier treatment of the country's
several million doubters—vague believers in a vague deity—and outright
unbelievers. What *was* noteworthy was that Nixon's statement caused
scarcely a ripple anywhere. No newspaper or magazine or public figure
seemed to think it worth while to take a stand for the political rights of atheists, agnostics, and freethinkers, who were being casually put beyond the
pale, as though the Constitution sanctioned their exclusion and national tradition hallowed it. Both these propositions are baseless. That they can even
be implied is a measure of how far we have slipped from the forthright ways
of the founding fathers.

After 174 years it should hardly have to be said that the Constitution,
far from providing a religious test for public office, expressly forbids any
such requirement. Yet the Supreme Court had to say it again only last June,
when it came to the rescue of a would-be notary public in Maryland. The as-
piration of one Roy R. Torcaso to witness signatures in Montgomery County had come up against a provision of the Maryland Constitution which
read: "No religious test ought ever to be required as a qualification for any
office of profit or trust in this state"—and then came the sleeper—"other
than a declaration of belief in the existence of God." Having no such belief,
Mr. Torcaso refused to sign the required declaration. That act of honesty
might have recommended him as a functionary whose job was to bear wit-

ness, since without fear of hell or expectation of heaven he could easily have lied. Firm believers have been known to do so from time to time. But under the law, Torcaso was rejected.

On appeal, the state's highest court ruled against him on the ground that Maryland's tradition of religious toleration was not "thought to encompass the ungodly," and the case then went up to the United States Supreme Court. That body ruled unanimously that Maryland's "religious test for public office unconstitutionally invades . . . . freedom of belief and religion."

In view of the clarity of the Constitution on this subject, it may be something of a surprise that Maryland was not alone in exacting a statement of faith from those who would hold public office. At the time, Arkansas, Mississippi, North Carolina, Pennsylvania, South Carolina, and Texas had similar provisions, and Tennessee went them one better. It not only required a belief in a Supreme Being, which would let in even those vague deists whose prayers might be addressed TO WHOM IT MAY CONCERN; it demanded, more specifically, a belief in "a future state of rewards and punishments." That would eliminate all those Unitarians, Jews, and Protestants of various shades who believe in God, but whose vision of the hereafter is not quite so graphic.

The opinion of many constitutional lawyers is that with the Supreme Court's decision, those particular laws became dead letters, whether or not they have yet been formally revoked. But the decision by no means removed all the disabilities under which nonbelieving Americans are obliged to carry on. Eleven states call for official oaths ending with the phrase "So help me God," and congressional statutes require the same words for Federal jobholders—*except for the President of the United States.* His oath of office is prescribed in Article II of the Constitution itself, the only one so imposed, and in it, significantly, there is no reference to a Supreme Being.

Still other states have so-called blasphemy laws, forbidding the public casting of doubt on the fundamentals of religious belief, though such laws are very rarely invoked. And in a number of states atheists may not serve as either witnesses or jurors. As the Maryland law runs, a witness or juror must believe that he "will be held morally accountable for his acts, and be rewarded or punished therefor, either in this world or in the world to come." Contradictory testimony is nevertheless as common in Maryland as it is elsewhere, the threat of consequences in the next world notwithstanding.

Aside from these dubiously legal disabilities, the climate of opinion creates other handicaps for the purely agnostic. A student at the University of Miami in Florida is dropped from a course for teachers because the county where he is to do his intern teaching will not allow the three R's to be imparted by an unbeliever. A New York couple professing no religion will find it impossible to adopt a child through the public channels. . . .

Illustrating the limbo to which avowed skeptics are assigned, the mayor of a New England city not long ago refused to accept a statue of Thomas

Paine because that patriot's religious views were, to say the least, controversial. In the same vein the Post Office Department has never brought out a Paine commemorative stamp, though it has paid philatelic honors to Joel Chandler Harris, Virginia Dare, the Pony Express, and the American Poultry Industry. Strenuous representations in Paine's behalf have been made repeatedly before Congressional committees and Post Office officials, but the man whose immeasurable service to the Revolution won tributes from Washington, Franklin, Adams and Jefferson is remembered by some Americans only as a free-thinker—and we are not so liberal about that sort of thing in the 1960's as they were in the 1790's.

The Torcaso affair served only to point up this fact. Seemingly jolted by the Supreme Court's opinion, a prominent newspaper columnist suggested that the justices had misinterpreted the intention of the founding fathers. "Is it clear," he asked incredulously, that they "wanted to make it possible for atheists to hold office and to conduct the affairs of their fellow men?"

The founders of the American Republic were men of their times, and their times were saturated with rationalism. As de Tocqueville, the great French observer of our young nation, observed, "The men of our days are naturally little disposed to believe." Paine and Jefferson were products of the Age of Reason. Franklin's great biographer, Carl Van Doren, characterized him as a "pagan skeptic." And the influence of the period was not lost on Washington or Adams either. The prevailing spirit among them was that of deism. Forerunners of modern Unitarianism, the deists were selective concerning the Bible—insofar as they accepted it at all—and they believed a Supreme Being to be vaguely inherent in Nature but very different from the personal God of the Scriptures. They thought that in any case men had to determine for themselves a basis for rational morality, and they had little use for theology or the ceremonials of organized religion. . . .

Jefferson was not so rough on the Bible as Paine, but John Quincy Adams wrote of him, "If not an absolute atheist, he had no belief in a future existence." That may be strong, but he advised a nephew to apply critical tests to the New Testament because "Your own reason is the only oracle given you by Heaven, and you are answerable for, not the rightness, but the uprightness of the decision."

Writing to Jefferson in the twilight of their lives, John Adams, who was a Unitarian, remarked that after a lifetime of reading polemics, "I have learned nothing of importance to me, for they have made no change in my moral or religious creed, which has for fifty or sixty years been contained in four short words, "Be just and good.""

I cite these few quotations only to show that a fairy relaxed and freewheeling attitude in matters of religion marked our ancestors, in contrast to the rigid conventionality of their political descendants.

What is more, their tradition of freedom prevailed down to the early days of this century. Although I shall not attempt here to characterize the much argued beliefs of Abraham Lincoln, they would not have qualified him for any Sunday-school awards. His law partner Herndon may have put it extremely—"As to Mr. Lincoln's religious views, he was, in short, an infidel." But it is true that as a young man he turned out an essay critically dissecting the Bible, which friends persuaded him to throw into the stove for the sake of his budding political career.

The generally pious post-Civil War era easily adjusted itself to a flood of unorthodoxy from its greatest literary representatives. Twain, Whitman, Poe, Emerson, Howells and Holmes ranged from an exuberant naturalism to a completely rationalist agnosticism. Above all, the Gilded Age saw the phenomenon of Robert G. Ingersoll. Here was a man who not only rejected religion but toured the country preaching the gospel of the unbeliever. "Our fathers retired Jehovah from politics," he would say. He particularly extolled Paine, "whose arguments were so good that his reputation got bad."

Yet Ingersoll enjoyed a brilliant career and reputation. Besides being the finest orator of his age, and one of the wittiest, he was among the most popular. Overflow audiences flocked to hear him "tell the truth about the Bible."

A colonel of Union cavalry at Shiloh and later attorney general of Illinois, Ingersoll was so highly regarded in Republican Party circles that he was chosen to put James G. Blaine in nomination for the Presidency, the occasion on which the candidate responded with his historic "plumed knight" speech. No one seemed to think the choice of the "great agnostic" an odd one, though such an endorsement now would surely be regarded as a kiss of death for any politican. When Ingersoll died, he was eulogized by the nation's great—Mark Twain and Andrew Carnegie among them—and he was buried in Arlington Cemetery.

It is hard to imagine a career like Ingersoll's in these timid days, though as recently as the '20's men like H. L. Mencken and Clarence Darrow still blared forth their unbelief. Sinclair Lewis went to the adolescent extent of challenging God to strike him dead in fifteen minutes in order to prove His existence. In science, Burroughs, Burbank, Edison, and Steinmetz were all unbelievers. Edison, who was exceedingly blunt on the subject, even helped finance the Freethinkers of America, an organization that is still struggling along.

Today, by contrast, a public man who publicly doubts is regarded as a shady figure. If in politics, he is much surer of being replaced at the next election than if he had been caught with his fist in the treasury. For aside from being "unpatriotic," agnosticism is "immoral." "If an officeholder doesn't believe in God, he may or may not be a person who believes in honesty or morality," says the columnist already cited. "He might not accept the Ten Commandments, for example, as necessarily governing his conduct."

Here, I submit, the would-be censor of belief is on even trickier ground than in his appeal to history. Obviously if an atheist who aspired to office were in fact immoral, perjury would be the last thing to upset him, and the gesture of belief would be enough to meet all requirements. Since one cannot be sure about a candidate's morality no matter how many oaths he takes, the question arises as to whether it is morality that is really being called for or merely conformity.

Whether or not one agrees with Shaw that man possesses a "natural sense of honor" that is "quite independent of religious instruction," it is impossible to accept the view that questioning spirits like Socrates, Spinoza and Giordano Bruno were less moral than their persecutors. Or to argue that the great abolitionists, William Lloyd Garrison and Wendell Phillips, neither of whom belonged to a church, needed lessons in virtue from pious churchgoers who bought and sold human beings at auction.

In the end if the state can demand officially—or public opinion unofficially—that officeholders acknowledge a conventional religious belief, then state and public are entitled to examine credentials. They are entitled to demand that a candidate's conviction be genuine, not just a matter of political convenience. And there's the rub. For who is to be entrusted with the inquisition required to winnow out the real from the synthetic in religious conviction? Happily the thought is preposterous as well as illegal.

Yet to exact a hollow profession of belief, Jefferson said, serves "only to beget habits of hypocrisy and meanness. . . ." And he has been proved right. Few political reporters would be at a loss to name men who, on entering public life, have suddenly felt the urge to appear in church for the first time since childhood. Paine understood the problem well, and his advice is as pertinent now as it ever was: ". . . it is necessary to the happiness of man that he be mentally faithful to himself. Infidelity does not consist in believing or in disbelieving; it consists in professing to believe what he does not believe." That is where the dry rot begins. In short, it is not the avowed agnostic who threatens the health of a society, nor the devout believer. It is the religious communicant who does not mean what he says, who uses religion to maintain his status or advance his career; and who, having in reality little or no faith himself, demands it all the more loudly of others.

*   *   *

Another intriguing question arises over what constitutes a fraudulent denomination. Who is to decide the authenticity of a set of religious beliefs? Such a question occurred in a case involving allegedly improper use of the mails to solicit money. The Ballard family, organizers of the "I Am" movement, claimed to be in direct communication with Jesus and appealed to the public for funds. They were prosecuted by the federal government, and in 1944 *United States v. Ballard* reached the Supreme Court. The basic problem in the prosecution of the sect was that, although religious beliefs could not justify criminal activity, how could the government prove that their religious claims were fraudulent when, based upon the establishment clause, the state could not recognize or deny any religious truths? The Court reversed conviction on just that ground: "Man's relation to his God was made no concern of the state. . . . The religious views espoused by respondents might seem incredible, if not preposterous, to most people. But if those doctrines are subject to trial before a jury charged with finding their truth or falsity, then the same can be done with the religious beliefs of any sect. When the triers of fact undertake that task, they enter a forbidden domain."

Another example of the state trying to make individuals go against their beliefs concerned the Amish. These are the so-called "plain folk," who have clung for centuries to their traditional religious-centered rural way of life, first in Pennsylvania and then elsewhere as well. For a number of years they have fought against state compulsory school laws on the grounds that attending high school takes their children out of a protected environment and exposes them to modern and corrupting influences which can destroy the social fabric of the religious community. The case of *Wisconsin v. Yoder,* decided in 1972, grew out of an appeal from a Wisconsin court ruling which enacted a token fine of $5 each from several Amish parents who defied the state's requirement that children attend school until they were 16. Chief Justice Warren Burger held this to be a "severe interference with religious freedom." He found that, although the state has a valid interest in compulsory education in order to provide an educated citizenry and to prevent child labor, it had not shown a "compelling government interest" that warranted overriding the religious freedom of the Amish.

Some legal scholars consider the case a landmark in the interpretation of the free-exercise clause. It appears that a religious dissenter may be given wider latitude than those who rely on other First Amendment guarantees and that the pluralism of religious diversity is to be encouraged. Chief Justice Burger wrote in his opinion: "A way of life that is odd or even erratic but interferes with no rights or interests of others is not to be condemned because it is different."

The most dramatic conflict between state and church involved the Jehovah's Witnesses and the compulsory flag salute. Before it ended, two rarities occurred: first, the Supreme Court reversed itself in the span of a few short years; second, overt religious persecution occurred in the 20th century. A number of states had adopted compulsory flag salute statutes for the public schools. These were upheld in the courts, but were opposed by the Watch Tower Bible and Tract Society, or Jehovah's Witnesses, who believed that to engage in the ceremony violated the biblical injunction against bowing down to a graven image. The matter first came to a head when two children, who were Witnesses, were expelled from school for refusing to participate in the flag salute. The Supreme Court in *Minersville School District v. Gobitis* (1940) reversed the lower courts by an eight-to-one vote and upheld the statute. Associate Justice Felix Frankfurter ruled that, if state legislatures felt that the flag salute contributed to national unity, they had the right to require it. Religious freedom was not an absolute, and, if all children were obliged to participate, then no grounds for immunity existed for those who objected to it. He made clear that the Court was not holding that the compulsion was desirable or wise, but that it was constitutional. Within three years the Court reversed itself.

During the interval a shocking amount of persecution and violence in different parts of the country was perpetrated against the Witnesses because of their continued refusal to salute the flag, especially since the country was at war. Also during the interval, several of the justices had second thoughts, and several new justices were appointed to the Court. The new case that came before them arose from a resolution adopted by the West Virginia Board of Education which, prompted by the Gobitis case, established the flag salute as a requirement. Failure to conform would be an act of insubordination resulting in expulsion and the possible charge of delinquency against the offending child and the levying of a fine against the parents. Once again, Witnesses made an appeal against enforcement of the regulations. What was truly remarkable was not that the Court reversed itself, but that it did so during wartime when democracy was being threatened by totalitariansim and the very group involved in the case was distributing antiwar propaganda.

Associate Justice Robert Jackson delivered the majority opinion, from which the following selection is taken. What are the issues in the case as Jackson sees them? In what ways is he critical of the Gobitis decision? What observation does he make on the meaning of liberty and the significance of the Bill of Rights? On what grounds was the Barnette case decided? What significance do you find in the following statements: "Those who begin coercive elimination of dissent soon find themselves exterminating dissenters. Compulsory unification of opinion achieves only the unanimity of the graveyard." "If there is any fixed star in our constitutional constellation, it is that no official . . . can prescribe what shall be orthodox in . . . matters of opinion or force citizens to confess by word or act their faith therein."

West Virginia Board of Education v. Barnette (1943)

This case calls upon us to reconsider a precedent decision, as the Court throughout its history often has been required to do. Before turning to the Gobitis Case, however, it is desirable to notice certain characteristics by which this controversy is distintinguished.

The freedom asserted by these appellees does not bring them into collision with rights asserted by any other individual. It is such conflicts which most frequently require intervention of the State to determine where the rights of one end and those of another begin. But the refusal of these persons to participate in the ceremony does not interfere with or deny rights of others to do so. Nor is there any question in this case that their behavior is peaceable and orderly. The sole conflict is between authority and rights of the individual. The State asserts power to condition access to public education on making a prescribed sign and profession and at the same time to coerce attendance by punishing both parent and child. The latter stand on a right of self-determination in matters that touch individual opinion and personal attitude.

As the present Chief Justice said in dissent in the Gobitis Case, the State may "require teaching by instruction and study of all in our history and in the structure and organization of our government, including the guaranties of civil liberty, which tend to inspire patriotism and love of country." Here, however, we are dealing with a compulsion of students to declare a belief. They are not merely made acquainted with the flag salute so that they may be informed as to what it is or even what it means. The issue here is whether this slow and easily neglected route to aroused loyalties constitutionally may be short-cut by substituting a compulsory salute and slogan. . . .

There is no doubt that, in connection with the pledges, the flag salute is a form of utterance. Symbolism is a primitive but effective way of communicating ideas. The use of an emblem or flag to symbolize some system, idea, institution, or personality, is a short cut from mind to mind. Causes and nations, political parties, lodges and ecclesiastical groups seek to knit the loyalty of their followings to a flag or banner, a color or design. The State announces rank, function, and authority through crowns and maces, uniforms and black robes; the church speaks through the Cross, the Crucifix, the altar and shrine, and clerical raiment. Symbols of State often convey political ideas just as religious symbols come to convey theological ones. Associated with many of these symbols are appropriate gestures of acceptance or respect: a salute, a bowed or bared head, a bended knee. A person gets from a symbol the meaning he puts into it, and what is one man's comfort and inspiration is another's jest and scorn. . . .

It is also to be noted that the compulsory flag salute and pledge requires affirmation of a belief and an attitude of mind. It is not clear whether the regulation contemplates that pupils forego any contrary convictions of their own and become unwilling converts to the prescribed ceremony or whether it will be acceptable if they simulate assent by words without belief and by a gesture barren of meaning. It is now a commonplace that censorship or suppression of expression of opinion is tolerated by our Constitution only when the expression presents a clear and present danger of action of a kind the State is empowered to prevent and punish. It would seem that involuntary affirmation could be commanded only on even more immediate and urgent grounds than silence. But here the power of compulsion is invoked without any allegation that remaining passive during a flag salute ritual creates a clear and present danger that would justify an effort even to muffle expression. To sustain the compulsory flag salute we are required to say that a Bill of Rights which guards the individual's right to speak his own mind, left it open to public authorities to compel him to utter what is not in his mind. . . .

Nor does the issue as we see it turn on one's possession of particular religious views or the sincerity with which they are held. While religion supplies appellees' motive for enduring the discomforts of making the issue in this case, many citizens who do not share these religious views hold such a compulsory rite to infringe constitutional liberty of the individual. It is not necessary to inquire whether non-conformist beliefs will exempt from the duty to salute unless we first find power to make the salute a legal duty.

The Gobitis decision, however, *assumed,* as did the argument in that case and in this, that power exists in the State to impose the flag salute discipline upon school children in general. The Court only examined and rejected a claim based on religious beliefs of immunity from an unquestioned general rule. The question which underlies the flag salute controversy is whether such a ceremony so touching matters of opinion and political attitude may be imposed upon the individual by official authority under powers committed to any political organization under our Constitution. We examine rather than assume existence of this power and, against this broader definition of issues in this case, re-examine specific grounds assigned for the Gobitis decision. . . .

Government of limited power need not be anemic government. Assurance that rights are secure tends to diminish fear and jealousy of strong government, and by making us feel safe to live under it makes for its better support. Without promise of a limiting Bill of Rights it is doubtful if our Constitution could have mustered enough strength to enable its ratification. To enforce those rights today is not to choose weak government over strong government. It is only to adhere as a means of strength to individual freedom of mind in preference to officially disciplined uniformity for which history indicates a disappointing and disastrous end.

The subject now before us exemplifies this principle. Free public education, if faithful to the ideal of secular instruction and political neutrality, will not be partisan or enemy of any class, creed, party, or faction. If it is to impose any ideological discipline, however, each party or denomination must seek to control, or failing that, to weaken the influence of the educational system. Observance of the limitations of the Constitution will not weaken government in the field appropriate for its exercise.

It was also considered in the Gobitis Case that functions of educational officers in states, counties and school districts were such that to interfere with their authority "would in effect make us the school board for the country."

The Fourteenth Amendment, as now applied to the States, protects the citizen against the State itself and all of its creatures—Boards of Education not excepted. These have, of course, important, delicate, and highly discretionary functions, but none that they may not perform within the limits of the Bill of Rights. That they are educating the young for citizenship is reason for scrupulous protection of Constitutional freedoms of the individual, if we are not to strangle the free mind at its source and teach youth to discount important principles of our government as mere platitudes.

Such Boards are numerous and their territorial jurisdiction often small. But small and local authority may feel less sense of responsibility to the Constitution, and agencies of publicity may be less vigilant in calling it to account. The action of Congress in making flag observance voluntary and respecting the conscience of the objector in a matter so vital as raising the Army contrasts sharply with these local regulations in matters relatively trivial to the welfare of the nation. There are village tyrants as well as village Hampdens, but none who acts under color of law is beyond reach of the Constitution.

The Gobitis opinion reasoned that this is a field "where courts possess no marked and certainly no controlling competence," that it is committed to the legislatures as well as the courts to guard cherished liberties and that it is constitutionally appropriate to "fight out the wise use of legislative authority in the forum of public opinion and before legislative assemblies rather than to transfer such a contest to the judicial arena," since all the "effective means of inducing political changes are left free."

The very purpose of a Bill of Rights was to withdraw certain subjects from the vicissitudes of political controversy, to place them beyond the reach of majorities and officials and to establish them as legal principles to be applied by the courts. One's rights to life, liberty, and property, to free speech, a free press, freedom of worship and assembly, and other fundamental rights may not be submitted to vote; they depend on the outcome of no elections.

In weighing arguments of the parties it is important to distinguish between the due process clause of the Fourteenth Amendment as an instrument for transmitting the principles of the First Amendment and those cases in which it is applied for its own sake. The test of legislation which collides with the Fourteenth Amendment, because it also collides with the principles of the First, is much more definite than the test when only the Fourteenth is involved. Much of the vagueness of the due process clause disappears when the specific prohibitions of the First become its standard. The right of a State to regulate, for example, a public utility may well include, so far as the due process test is concerned, power to impose all of the restrictions which a legislature may have a "rational basis" for adopting. But freedoms of speech and of press, of assembly, and of worship may not be infringed on such slender grounds. They are susceptible of restriction only to prevent grave and immediate danger to interests which the state may lawfully protect. It is important to note that while it is the Fourteenth Amendment which bears directly upon the State it is the more specific limiting principles of the First Amendment that finally govern this case.

Nor does our duty to apply the Bill of Rights to assertions of official authority depend upon our possession of marked competence in the field where the invasion of rights occurs. True, the task of translating the majestic generalities of the Bill of Rights, conceived as part of the pattern of liberal government in the eighteenth century, into concrete restraints on officials dealing with the problems of the twentieth century, is one to disturb self-confidence. These principles grew in soil which also produced a philosophy that the individual was the center of society, that his liberty was attainable through mere absence of governmental restraints, and that government should be entrusted with few controls and only the mildest supervision over men's affairs. We must transplant these rights to a soil in which the laissez-faire concept or principle of non-interference has withered at least as to economic affairs, and social advancements are increasingly sought through closer integration of society and through expanded and strengthened governmental controls. These changed conditions often deprive precedents of reliability and cast us more than we would choose upon our own judgment. But we act in these matters not by authority of our competence but by force of our commissions. We cannot, because of modest estimates of our competence in such specialties as public education, withhold the judgment that history authenticates as the function of this Court when liberty is infringed.

Lastly, and this is the very heart of the Gobitis opinion, it reasons that "national unity is the basis of national security," that the authorities have "the right to select appropriate means for its attainment," and hence reaches the conclusion that such compulsory measures toward "national unity" are constitutional. Upon the verity of this assumption depends our answer in this case.

National unity as an end which officials may foster by persuasion and example is not in question. The problem is whether under our Constitution compulsion as here employed is a permissible means for its achievement.

Struggles to coerce uniformity of sentiment in support of some end thought essential to their time and country have been waged by many good as well as by evil men. Nationalism is a relatively recent phenomenon but at other times and places the ends have been racial or territorial security, support of a dynasty or regime, and particular plans for saving souls. As first and moderate methods to attain unity have failed, those bent on its accomplishment must resort to an ever increasing severity. As governmental pressure toward unity becomes greater, so strife becomes more bitter as to whose unity it shall be. Probably no deeper division of our people could proceed from any provocation than from finding it necessary to choose what doctrine and whose program public educational officials shall compel youth to unite in embracing. Ultimate futility of such attempts to compel coherence is the lesson of every such effort from the Roman drive to stamp our Christianity as a disturber of its pagan unity, the Inquisition, as a means to religious and dynastic unity, the Siberian exiles as a means to Russian unity, down to the fast failing efforts of our present totalitarian enemies. Those who begin coercive elimination of dissent soon find themselves exterminating dissenters. Compulsory unification of opinion achieves only the unanimity of the graveyard.

It seems trite but necessary to say that the First Amendment to our Constitution was designed to avoid these ends by avoiding these beginnings. There is no mysticism in the American concept of the State or of the nature or origin of its authority. We set up government by consent of the governed, and the Bill of Rights denies those in power any legal opportunity to coerce that consent. Authority here is to be controlled by public opinion, not public opinion by authority.

The case is made difficult not because the principles of its decision are obscure but because the flag involved is our own. Nevertheless, we apply the limitations of the Constitution with no fear that freedom to be intellectually and spiritually diverse or even contrary will disintegrate the social organization. To believe that patriotism will not flourish if patriotic ceremonies are voluntary and spontaneous instead of a compulsory routine is to make an unflattering estimate of the appeal of our institutions to free minds. We can have intellectual individualism and the rich cultural diversities that we owe to exceptional minds only at the price of occasional eccentricity and abnormal attitudes. When they are so harmless to others or to the State as those we deal with here, the price is not too great. But freedom to differ is not limited to things that do not matter much. That would be a mere shadow of freedom. The test of its substance is the right to differ as to things that touch the heart of the existing order.

If there is any fixed star in our constitutional constellation, it is that no official, high or petty, can prescribe what shall be orthodox in politics, nationalism, religion, or other matters of opinion or force citizens to confess by word or act their faith therein. If there are any circumstances which permit an exception, they do not now occur to us.

We think the action of the local authorities in compelling the flag salute and pledge transcends constitutional limitations on their power and invades the sphere of intellect and spirit which it is the purpose of the First Amendment to our Constitution to reserve from all official control.

The decision of this Court in Minersville School District v. Gobitis . . . [is] overruled, and the judgment enjoining enforcement of the West Virginia Regulation is affirmed.

*   *   *

In the same year as the Gobitis case the Supreme Court heard another case involving the Jehovah's Witnesses, *Cantwell v. Connecticut* (1940). The reason a significant number of cases on freedom of religion reaching the high court have involved the Witnesses is their willingness to undergo great expense to fight for their rights through the courts. The Cantwell case involved the door-to-door selling or free distribution of the *Watch Tower* and other tracts. The defendants had been found guilty of soliciting without a license and breach of the peace. The Supreme Court overturned the lower courts on grounds of violating the First Amendment: "To condition the solicitation of aid for the perpetuation of religious views or systems upon a license, the grant of which rests in the exercise of a determination by state authority as to what is a religious cause, is to lay a forbidden burden upon the exercise of liberty protected by the Constitution."

The importance of *Cantwell* lies in the Court's decision finally and firmly to establish the inclusion of religion as one of the freedoms protected by the Fourteenth Amendment: "The fundamental concept of liberty embodied in that Amendment embraces the liberties guaranteed by the First Amendment. The First Amendment declares that Congress shall make no law respecting an establishment of religion or prohibiting the free exercise thereof. The Fourteenth Amendment has rendered the legislatures of the states as incompetent as Congress to enact such laws."

Freedom of Conduct

As with political action compared to political belief and expression, religious action has been subject to more limitations than have religious belief and expression. This involves both conduct required by religion but prohibited by the state and conduct called for by the state but forbidden by religion. One example examined in a previous chapter dealt with the Mormons and their practice of polygamy. But generally, the issues involved are more complex and difficult to resolve.

One issue of perennial interest, even though it directly involves only a small proportion of the American people, is the Sunday closing law. Sabbath restrictions have existed since earliest colonial times and persist in much attenuated form to the present. Most restrictions on recreation, amusements, and sporting events are gone, but to this day many businesses are forbidden by state law and local ordinance from being open on the Christian Sabbath. This works a particular hardship on orthodox Jews who observe a different Sabbath, and who, if they are businessmen, are placed at an economic disadvantage. Apart from this, some people maintain that although some features of Sunday closing laws may be desirable on nonreligious grounds, they should all be repealed. They contend that Sabbath laws violate religious freedom for both Christians and non-Christians, since they are forced by the state to conduct their affairs in conformity with particular ritualistic principles.

Although the Supreme Court had dealt with this conflict earlier, in 1961 it found itself acting on four cases in one year. Two of them warrant examination. In *McGowan v. Maryland,* the Court acknowledged that original Sunday laws were motivated by religious forces, but they had increasingly taken on a secular motivation and emphasis, to the point where they no longer constituted an establishment of religion. "The present purpose and effect of most of them is to provide a uniform day of rest for all citizens; the fact that this day is Sunday, a day of particular significance for the dominant Christian sects, does not bar the State from achieving its secular goals." In response to the question why the day was specified instead of allowing it to be a matter of personal choice, the Court agreed that it should be one that could be shared by the community; also the law would be more readily enforced. It was declared that state action which serves a sound public purpose does not become unconstitutional because it happens also to serve the purpose of a religious group.

In *Braunfeld v. Brown,* the issue was more narrowly drawn. Of the 34 states that had Sabbath laws, 21 had a discretionary feature which exempted from Sunday closing those who observed another day of rest. Pennsylvania, not one of the 21, was being sued in this case. The Court found that the absence of an exemption was not a violation of free exercise. The burden on religion was indirect since the merchants involved did not have to choose between following their faith and obeying the law. They could close on both Sunday and their own Sabbath, thereby being economically disadvantaged by their own choice. Justices Douglas, Brennan, and Stewart vigorously dissented. They felt it was an unfair choice and that the states without discretionary features could undergo the slight administrative inconvenience that the other states were under.

Two years later, in a related case, *Sherbert v. Verner* (1963), the Court seemed to modify its position. This involved a Seventh Day Adventist who was fired from her job because she would not work on Saturday, her Sabbath. She was refused unemployment compensation by her state on the grounds that she refused to work when work was available to her. The majority now held that this action was as heavy a burden as a fine for Saturday worship and therefore violated freedom of religion.

A form of conduct required by the state but forbidden by religion, at least some religions, that has received continued attention by Congress and the courts for more than half a century and stirred up much controversy, especially in recent years, is compulsory service in the armed forces. Those who seek and receive exemption from this obligation on religious grounds are classified as conscientious objectors. As will be shown, however, the courts have not to date recognized the exemption on First Amendment grounds.

The Selective Service Act of 1917 contained the provision that a person could not be compelled to serve in the armed forces if he is "a member of any well-recognized religious sect or organization . . . whose existing creed or principles forbid its members to participate in war in any form and whose religious convictions are against war or participation therein." This exemption was aimed primarily at traditional pacifist sects like the Quakers and Mennonites. It was upheld by the Supreme Court in *United States v. Macintosh* (1931), but the opinion clearly defined its limited source:

> The conscientious objector is relieved from the obligation to bear arms in obedience to no constitutional provision, express or implied; but because, and only because, it has accorded with the policy of Congress thus to relieve him. . . . The privilege . . . to avoid bearing arms comes, not from the Constitution, but from the acts of Congress. That body may grant or withhold the exemption as in its wisdom it sees fit; and, if it be withheld, the . . . conscientious objector cannot successfully assert the privilege.

Because this original exemption was predicated on membership in a religious group that forbade military service, the government was open to the charge that this stipulation represented a preference of some religions over others, a violation of the doctrine of separation. To avoid this, when the first peacetime draft was adopted by Congress in 1940, the exemption was broadened to include anyone who objected to "participation in war in any form" by "reason of religious training and belief." However, the law specifically excluded those whose objections were nonreligious and based on a "political and social philosophy." Following World War II, the exemption was narrowed once more by the requirement that religious training and belief include "an individual's belief in a relation to a Supreme Being involving duties superior to those arising from any human relation, but does not include essentially political, sociological or philosophical views or a merely personal moral code." This provision was designed to exclude agnostics and atheists.

What Congress thought was a tightening of regulations concerning conscientious objection turned out to have the opposite effect. For the stipulation of a belief in a Supreme Being ran the danger of being considered a classification by government of different religions, a clear violation of the First Amendment. The issue came before the Supreme Court in 1965 in *United States v. Seeger,* which involved the conviction of several conscientious objectors for refusal to be inducted into the armed forces. Each of them had filed for objector's status but either left unanswered the portion of the form asking about their belief in a Supreme Being or wrote in an explanation of their beliefs. Seeger showed a disbelief in God, "except in the remotest sense," but expressed a "belief in and devotion to goodness and virtue for their own sakes, and a religious faith in a purely ethical creed." The case was appealed from lower federal courts, and the unanimous opinion was written by Associate Justice Tom Clark. How does he define the legal issues involved? What is there about religion and its status in the country at present which makes the task of determining eligibility for conscientious objector status so difficult? What test is proposed? Why is it found that Seeger met the test?

United States v. Seeger (1965)

The crux of the problem lies in the phrase "religious training and belief" which Congress has defined as "belief in a relation to a Supreme Being involving duties superior to those arising from any human relation." In assigning meaning to this statutory language we may narrow the inquiry by noting briefly those scruples expressly excepted from the definition. The section excludes those persons who, disavowing religious belief, decide on the basis of essentially political, sociological or economic considerations that war is wrong and that they will have no part of it. These judgments have historically been reserved for the Government, and in matters which can be said to fall within these areas the conviction of the individual has never been permitted to override that of the State. The statute further excludes those whose opposition to war stems from a "merely personal moral code," a phrase to which we shall have occasion to turn later in discussing the application of section 6 (j) [of the Selective Service Act of 1948] to these cases. We also pause to take note of what is not involved in this litigation. No party claims to be an atheist or attacks the statute on this ground. The question is not, therefore, one between theistic and atheistic beliefs. We do not deal with or intimate any decision on that situation in these cases. Nor do the parties claim the monotheistic belief that there is but one God; what they claim (with the possible exception of Seeger who bases his position here not on factual but on purely constitutional grounds) is that they adhere to theism, which is the "Belief in the existence of a god or gods; . . . Belief in superhuman powers or spiritual agencies in one or many gods," as opposed to atheism. Our question, therefore, is the narrow one: Does the term "Supreme Being" as used in section 6 (j) mean the orthodox God or the broader concept of a power or being, or a faith, "to which all else is subordinate or upon which all else is ultimately dependent"? Webster's New International Dictionary, (Second Edition). In considering this question we resolve it solely in relation to the language of section 6 (j) and not otherwise.

Few would quarrel, we think, with the proposition that in no field of human endeavor has the tool of language proved so inadequate in the communication of ideas as it has in dealing with the fundamental questions of man's predicament in life, in death or in final judgment and retribution. This fact makes the task of discerning the intent of Congress in using the phrase "Supreme Being" a complex one. Nor is it made the easier by the richness and variety of spiritual life in our country. Over 250 sects inhabit our land. Some believe in a purely personal God, some in a supernatural deity; others think of religion as a way of life envisioning as its ultimate goal the day when all men can live together in perfect understanding and peace. There are those who think of God as the depth of our being; others, such as the Buddhists, strive for a state of lasting rest through self-denial and inner purification; in Hindu philosophy, the Supreme Being is the transcendental reality which is truth, knowledge and bliss. Even those religious groups who have traditionally opposed war in every form have splintered into various denominations. . . . This vast panoply of beliefs reveals the magnitude of the problem which faced the Congress when it set about providing an exemption from armed service. It also emphasizes the care that Congress realized was necessary in the fashioning of an exemption which would be in keeping with its long-established policy of not picking and choosing among religious beliefs.

In spite of the elusive nature of the inquiry, we are not without certain guidelines. In amending the 1940 Act, Congress adopted almost intact the language of Chief Justice Hughes in the *United States v. Macintosh, supra*:

> The essence of religion is belief in a relation to God involving duties superior to those arising from any human relation.

By comparing the statutory definition with those words, however, it becomes readily apparent that the Congress deliberately broadened them by substituting the phrase "Supreme Being" for the appellation "God." And in so doing it is also significant that Congress did not elaborate on the form or nature of this higher authority which it chose to designate as "Supreme Being." . . .

Moreover, the Senate Report on the bill specifically states that section 6 (j) was intended to re-enact "substantially the same provisions as were found" in the 1940 Act. That statute, of course, refers to "religious training and belief" without more. Admittedly, all of the parties here purport to base their objection on religious belief. It appears, therefore, that we need only look to this clear statement of congressional intent as set out in the report. Under the 1940 Act it was necessary only to have a conviction based upon religious training and belief; we believe that is all that is required here. Within that phrase would come all sincere religious beliefs which are based upon a power or being, or upon a faith, to which all else is subordinate or upon which all else is ultimately dependent. The test might be stated in these words: A sincere and meaningful belief which occupies in the life of its possessor a place parallel to that filled by the God of those admittedly qualifying for the exemption comes within the statutory definition. This construction avoids imputing to Congress an intent to classify different religious beliefs, exempting some and excluding others, and is in accord with the well-established congressional policy of equal treatment for those whose opposition to service is grounded in their religious tenets. . . .

As we noted earlier, the statutory definition excepts those registrants whose beliefs are based on a "merely personal moral code." The records in these cases, however, show that at no time did any one of the applicants suggest that his objection was based on a "merely personal moral code." Indeed at the outset each of them claimed in his application that his objection was based on a religious belief. We have construed the statutory definition broadly and it follows that any exception to it must be interpreted narrowly. The use by Congress of the words "merely personal" seems to us to restrict the exception to a moral code which is not only personal but which is the sole basis for the registrant's belief and is in no way related to a Supreme Being. It follows, therefore, that if the claimed religious beliefs of the respective registrants in these cases meet the test that we lay down then their objections cannot be based on a "merely personal" moral code.

In *Seeger*, No. 50, the Court of Appeals failed to find sufficient "externally compelled beliefs." However, it did find that "it would seem impossible to say with assurance that [Seeger] is not bowing to 'external commands' in virtually the same sense as is the objector who defers to the will of a supernatural power." . . . Of course, as we have said, the statute does not distinguish between externally and internally derived beliefs. Such a determination would, as the Court of Appeals observed, prove impossible as a practical matter, and we have found that Congress intended no such distinction.

The Court of Appeals also found that there was no question of the applicant's sincerity. He was a product of a devout Roman Catholic home; he was a close student of Quaker beliefs from which he said "much of [his] thought is derived"; he approved of their opposition to war in any form; he devoted his spare hours to the American Friends Service Committee and was assigned to hospital duty.

In summary, Seeger professed "religious belief" and "religious faith." He did not disavow any belief "in a relation to a Supreme Being"; indeed he stated that "the cosmic order does, perhaps, suggest a creative intelligence." He decried the tremendous "spiritual" price man must pay for his willingness to destroy human life. In light of his beliefs and the unquestioned sincerity with which he held them, we think the Board, had it applied the test we propose today, would have granted him the exemption. We think it clear that the beliefs which prompted his objection occupy the same place in his life as the belief in a traditional deity holds in the lives of his friends, the Quakers. We are reminded once more of Dr. Tillich's thoughts:

> And if that word [God] has not much meaning for you, translate it, and speak of the depths of your life, of the source of your being, of your ultimate concern, *of what you take seriously without any reservation.* Perhaps, in order to do so, you must forget everything traditional that you have learned about God. . . .

It may be that Seeger did not clearly demonstrate what his beliefs were with regard to the usual understanding of the term "Supreme Being." But as we have said Congress did not intend that to be the test. We therefore affirm the judgment in No. 50.

*   *   *

Postscript

It took the ingenuity of the Court to avoid striking down the conscientious objection provisions of the draft as being unconstitutional or ruling that the exemption was limited to those who held orthodox religious beliefs. Congress, however, was not inclined to tolerate such a liberal interpretation of eligibility. By 1967, when the Selective Service Act came up for renewal, opposition to the war in Vietnam had greatly expanded the number who sought objector status. The new law did not contain the Supreme Being clause. But it was now a case of locking the barn door after the horse had escaped.

The very next year a lower federal court citing the Seeger decision held that a self-designated atheist qualified as a conscientious objector because his beliefs in a "man's mortal soul" and in the sinfulness of killing were clearly "a product of a faith." This anticipated by two years *Welch v. United States* (1970) in which the Supreme Court found that any strong belief that killing in war was immoral and forbidden by conscience was equivalent to religious belief. Justice Black's opinion held that a draft registrant may not be the best judge of whether his own beliefs are religious or nonreligious, because he might not be aware of the broad scope of the term "religious." The Justice concluded: "That section [of the Selective Service Act] exempts from military service all those whose consciences, spurred by deeply held moral, ethical, or religious beliefs, would give them no rest or peace if they allowed themselves to become a part of an instrument of war."

Because of the controversial nature of the Vietnam conflict and the efforts of countless numbers of young men to avoid the draft, a special aspect of exemption from service arose, creating a tremendous furor in the late 1960s and early 1970s—selective conscientious objection or objection to a particular war. Its adherents maintained that they would not object to serving in the armed forces in other circumstances, but because the conflict in Southeast Asia was immoral they sought objector's status. Those who supported this exemption based it upon the concept of a "just war" (as contrasted to unjust war), first advanced for Christians by St. Augustine in the 5th century. The Supreme Court confronted the issue in 1971 in *Gillette v. United States* when it barred the exemption. In examining the Military Service Act, it found that Congress limited it to those who are "opposed to participation in war in any form." This means that those who object to military service in a particular war, even though their objection is religious and sincere, may be denied exemption without violating their religious freedom. This is where the situation stands today.

Questions

1. What evidence can you find from recent local or national campaign speeches and literature to support or contradict Bendiner's thesis about religion and politics?
2. Why do you feel that religious belief is or is not a valid defense against violating the law?
3. Although no one can "second guess" the Supreme Court with any predictable accuracy, everyone is free to try. In light of the decision in *Wisconsin v. Yoder* (1972), what do you believe the Court's position would be today if it had before it the question of Mormon polygamy?
4. What, if any, Sabbath restrictions exist in your community or state?
5. How do you feel the broad issue of conscientious objection and the specific question of selective objection should be dealt with by Congress and the courts?

Suggested Readings

Issues of free exercise are dealt with in:

Albornoz, Carillo de. *The Basis of Religious Liberty*. New York: Association Press, 1963.

Ballou, Adin. *Christian Non-Resistance*. Philadelphia, 1910 (DaCapo Press Reprint).

Herberg, Will. *Protestant-Catholic-Jew*. Garden City, N.Y.: Doubleday & Co., 1955.

Kurland, Philip. *Religion and the Law*. Chicago: Aldine Publishing Co., 1962.

Manwaring, David. *Render Unto Caesar: The Flag Salute Controversy*. Chicago: University of Chicago Press, 1962.

Stokes, Anson, and Pfeffer, Leo. *Church and State in the United States*. New York: Harper & Row, 1961.

Sweet, William. *Religion in the Development of American Culture*. New York: Charles Scribner's Sons, 1952.

7. A Wall of Separation

The place of religion in our society is an exalted one, achieved through a long tradition of reliance on the home, the church and the inviolable citadel of the individual heart and mind. We have come to recognize through bitter experience that it is not written within the power of government to invade the citadel, whether its purpose or effect be to aid or oppose, to advance or retard. In the relationship between man and religion, the state is firmly committed to a position of neutrality.

—*Abington School District v. Schempp*

There is a marked difference between principle and practice as far as religious freedom is concerned, much more so in respect to the establishment clause than to free exercise. Although the United States is a secular nation, the public has throughout its history insisted upon expressions of religiosity both by elected officials and by agencies of government. Religious mottoes on stamps, coins, and currency; the opening of congressional, legislative, and judicial sessions with prayer; tax-supported chaplains in Congress and the armed forces; presidential proclamations on religious holidays; religious services in the White House; Christmas displays on public buildings —these and many others serve to illustrate the point. In the 1950s, Congress amended the Pledge of Allegiance to include the words "under God" and required that all currency contain the motto "In God We Trust."

However, religious observances have been most evident in public education. The assumption of responsibility for education by the state and its secularization were realized in the middle of the 19th century. Nevertheless, traces of its religious roots were retained in such practices as recitation of prayers and reading from the Bible, both in the Protestant form. These practices were continued down to the early 1960s, although not without challenge from various dissenting groups, both secular and religious. Another means of supporting religious beliefs in the public schools came into being during the 20th century with the introduction into many systems of a practice known as released time.

Legal scholars find that the most pressing current problem and greatest controversy involving church-state relations is with religious education and the degree, if any, to which the state should support it or be involved in the teaching of religious concepts. Some religions favor the inculcation of religious precepts in the public schools. Others believe that religious teachings should pervade the entire school curriculum on a regular basis and for this purpose have developed parochial schools. In recent years, parochial systems increasingly have been advocating direct or indirect financial assistance from the state for their programs. Although the issue of religion in the public schools has been emotionally charged and has given rise to several very important Supreme Court cases, the controversy over public support for religious schools has been persistent and significant.

Public Aid

There is no question that the First Amendment prohibits the use of federal funds, and it, along with the Fourteenth Amendment, prohibits the use of state funds for religious denominations or religious purposes. The problem arises over grants to sectarian-controlled institutions such as hospitals, nursing homes, orphanages, as well as schools, and the use by them of public facilities. When are they permissible, and at what point do they transgress the Constitution? Further difficulty in achieving clarification arises over the hesitance of individuals to incur community displeasure by bringing the issue to court, the lack of legal standing, until recently, of such an individual to sue, and the general unwillingness of lower courts to strike down most practices.

Complex Controversies

Before we examine the subject of aid to religious schools, several basic facts need first to be recognized. First, sectarian schools serve the public interest by providing the facilities and curriculums required by compulsory education laws. Second, they exist not by state permission but by constitutional right as recognized by the Supreme Court in *Pierce v. Society of Sisters* (1925), examined earlier. Third, a democratically pluralistic society is one that maximizes choice; in this case, parents have the alternative of sending their children to public, secular private, or sectarian schools. This last category is commonly referred to as parochial.

Although parochial schools are maintained by several Protestant denominations, Orthodox Jewry, and the Roman Catholic Church, the Catholic system enrolls four-fifths of the total and, consequently, the controversy that exists revolves around it. Catholic parochial schools came into existence as a result of the large immigration of the Irish in the mid-19th century. They were instructed by the Church to establish religious schools in order to preserve their faith. Nevertheless, evidence shows that many sent their children to the public schools and would have kept them there if they had not encountered nativistic hostility and the compulsory participation in Protestant prayers, hymns, and Bible reading in the classroom. Once they set up their own schools, they demanded public support for them. Stymied in their efforts, they then exerted pressure to transform the public schools into completely secular institutions to safeguard those Catholic children who attended them. From the post-Civil War period to World War II, Catholics supported and flourished under separation of church and state.

However, under the financial strain of maintaining a larger and larger parochial system, they began once again to demand some form of public assistance. The issue has come to a head during the last 25 years, principally for two reasons. One has been the rapidly mounting costs of all forms of education, something which has hit parochial schools particularly hard. A marked decline in number of low-paid religious faculty and the increased use of lay teachers has been accompanied by a greater demand by Catholic parents for better education for their children through smaller classes and more costly curricular offerings. In the last few years these factors have constituted a huge financial drain, contributing to the closing of more and more parish facilities. In the mid-1960s, there were 5.6 million pupils in Catholic elementary and secondary schools, representing about 15 percent of the nation's total enrollment. By 1970, the number had dropped to 4.8 million, and at present, it is below 4 million. The second reason for controversy has been the expanded role of schools in providing social services not traditionally considered part of education and the growing assumption by the federal government of financial responsibility for a number of them.

An examination of the status of parochial education in the country reveals a complex situation. While it is true that a significant number of schools are closing down or consolidating, this is true mainly in the inner cities from which middle-class Irish and Italian Catholics have moved. However, there is a drop nationwide in the total number of children attending sectarian schools, particularly on the elementary level. As Catholics have become less of a minority, both in numbers and in power, and their concern over Protestantization has disappeared, the need for a separate system has diminished. Furthermore, larger numbers of Catholic parents are questioning the effectiveness of parochial education altogether. Be that as it may, pressure for public aid continues unabated.

Public aid to religious education became a controversial public issue shortly after World War II, when Congress launched an intensive effort to establish a broad program of federal aid. It was to be confined strictly to the public schools. This aroused the ire of the Catholic hierarchy, which was able to block the adoption of any measure excluding their schools. Ever since, proposals for broad federal aid have foundered on this issue. Opponents of parochial aid refuse to include nonpublic schools as beneficiaries, and proponents block bills excluding private schools. Shortly after taking office, President John F. Kennedy called for a carefully developed legal opinion on the subject from the Department of Health, Education, and Welfare, which found that parochial aid would be unconstitutional. This caused Kennedy to take a strong position against it. Nevertheless, the fact that the controversy continues makes it worth while to examine the views of the two sides. Before we list them, it should be noted that although there are exceptions, the major religions divide sharply on the issue. Protestants and Jews (with the exception of Orthodox Jewry) generally oppose federal aid to parochial schools, whereas Roman Catholics favor it.

The principal arguments in favor of government aid to religious education are:

1. The nation has always had a strong religious tradition, and public support of religions in fulfilling their purpose of educating their youthful adherents is consistent with this tradition. There is no violation of the doctrine of separation as long as the aid is available to all.
2. Public funds have been used for religious education for some time. The school-lunch program, the G.I. Bill of Rights, the National Defense Education Act, the Higher Education Facilities Act, the Economic Opportunity Act, and the Elementary and Secondary Education Act have all embraced parochial schools or colleges.
3. Parochial schools provide instruction for their pupils in secular subjects as well as religious ones, thus "performing a public function" by providing a service which relieves the public schools of part of their burden. Why should the public not pay for this?
4. Parents who send their children to religious schools have to pay tuition as well as the taxes everyone pays for maintaining the public school system. This is a form of double taxation and is patently unfair.
5. The shortages of funds experienced by public systems throughout the country to carry out traditional functions and the newer demands made of education are also being experienced by the parochial schools. In fact, their financial straits are even worse, since the decline in numbers of religious sisters necessitates employing higher paid lay teachers.
6. Programs designed to provide for the welfare of children, such as hot lunches, transportation, medical checkups, and remedial services, are for the benefit of children. What difference does it make if those involved attend sectarian or secular institutions?

The principal arguments against aid are:

1. Any form of aid is a violation of the historic doctrine of separation even if nonpreferential. However, aid to religious education is actually preferential, since in many instances parochial schools exclude nonadherents from admission, employment, and involvement in school policies, and the overwhelming preponderance of them are Catholic.

2. If state aid is openly established, a great many more denominations will set up religious schools. This will result in a rivalry for funds, political pressure on public officials, and, most serious, the fragmentation of education and the ultimate destruction of the public school system.

3. It is a small step from aid for parochial schools to aid for other religious enterprises, and where the government's money goes, so is its control likely to follow. This could bring back the tragic entanglement of church and state from which the nation freed itself almost 200 years ago.

4. Since sectarian education separates children by religion and serves to thwart cultural unity, it is wrong for the state to encourage through financial support—although it has no right to prevent children from obtaining a religious education—a system that fosters divisiveness.

5. The double taxation claim is misleading on three counts. A tax is something that one is forced to pay, and since no one is forced to send his children to a religious school, he is not being "taxed." Secondly, unmarried and childless couples pay taxes to support public schools even though they, like parents who send their children to parochial schools, do not use them. Finally, the public schools do not exist just as a means for parents to educate their children: they serve society as a whole, and therefore all the public must support them.

6. Although parochial school children should be included in school lunch, medical, and other public welfare benefits, these programs should be administered under public auspices. Furthermore, child benefits should not be expanded into areas which are more educational than welfare such as transportation, textbooks, classroom equipment, and the salaries of teachers of secular subjects.

During the mid-1960s, President Lyndon B. Johnson and the Congress found a means of skirting the dilemma of federal aid for all or federal aid for none. In the Economic Opportunity Act of 1964 and the Elementary and Secondary Education Act of 1965, they focused on economically and culturally deprived children as beneficiaries of a number of federally funded training and education programs. Under the EOA, such instruments as the

Job Corps, the Neighborhood Youth Corps, Project Headstart, and VISTA were established and allowed to operate in cooperation with public and private (including religious) agencies such as schools, hospitals, and settlement houses. ESEA (the school act) provides funds for educational projects in low-income areas aimed at all educationally deprived children whether in public or parochial schools. This includes school libraries, textbooks, curriculum materials, audiovisual equipment, and the like. Although the law and the money are federal, ESEA is implemented on the local level, and it is here that violations of church-state separation have been reported and documented.

Another program that recently has become more widespread has been shared time or dual enrollment. This is the practice whereby parochial school children attend their own institutions for part of the day, where they are taught, along with religion, subjects deemed to require a spiritual treatment, such as literature and the social studies; the balance of their instruction in such subjects as mathematics, science, physical education, and foreign languages is obtained in the public schools.

A wide division exists between advocates and opponents of shared time on both its constitutionality and its social desirability. Some contend that it clearly violates separation of church and state because it involves government support of religion; others hold that it is clearly permissible, and some assert that it is mandatory. On social grounds, it is maintained that it would eliminate the need for federal aid to religious schools, would provide parochial children with public benefits available to others without using tax money for religious instruction, would lessen the pressure for religious exercises in the public schools, and would reduce community divisiveness and widen support of public education. On the other hand, it is contended that divisiveness would be worse because the parochial visitors would probably be kept in distinct groups and church-state conflicts would be brought down to the school level, administrative and scheduling problems would be great, any cooperative planning between public and parochial officials would violate the doctrine of separation, the public school system would be weakened if not destroyed, and it would not satisfy the orthodox who view spiritual education as a totality that cannot be segmented.

These diametrically opposing positions can be put in focus by their answers to one critical question. Would the advocates of shared time accept the proviso that such programs would be administered solely by public authorities, that they would serve public objectives, that parochial authorities could not control selection of such things as textbooks, instructors, and schools, and that the public benefits go not to the parochial schools but only to the children themselves while attending the public schools? If the answer is "yes," would this satisfy those who support sectarian education? If it is "no," then what of the establishment clause?

A further source of controversy over church-state relations in education occurs in higher education. Opinions differ over whether federal aid to colleges and universities is different from aid to lower levels, since higher education is not universal, free, compulsory, and available to all, and the students are more mature and less susceptible to religious indoctrination. One complicating factor is that private colleges are of different types: some, like New York University, Stanford, and Pennsylvania, are and have always been secular in origin and purpose; others, like Harvard, Princeton, and Columbia, were originally religious in nature but have evolved into totally secular institutions; still others, like Notre Dame, Holy Cross and Brigham Young, are and have always been sectarian in nature. Yet all are in desperate need of public support and probably could not survive without it. There is also ample precedent for including church-affiliated institutions; the various G.I. Bills of Rights and the National Defense Education Act of 1958 funneled large amounts of federal funds into all types of colleges.

As long as tax money is not used for schools of divinity, for chapels, or for direct religious instruction, some claim, then aid is constitutional. Others insist that aid under any of the following conditions would constitute a breach in the wall of separation: if membership in a particular religion was a requirement for employment of faculty or admission of students, if attendance at religious services or enrollment in a course on religion was compulsory, if students were subject to rules of conduct of a sectarian nature. However, nothing should prevent an institution from offering courses *about* religion or having a department of religion.

Judicial Distinctions

The positions taken by the courts on the issues raised by the different forms of aid to religious schools have been clear-cut in some respects and vague and ambivalent in others. They have ruled clearly that sectarian religious instruction has no place in the public schools and that tax money cannot be used to support parochial education. Nevertheless, in the last generation, many states have been providing free lunches, textbooks, bus transportation, and medical care to all schools, public and private, secular and sectarian. In *Cochran v. Louisiana* (1930), the Supreme Court first enunciated the "child benefit" doctrine, which holds that aid directed toward the benefit of children, irrespective of their religion, is designed to promote the public welfare and is, therefore, constitutional. In this case, a state's right to provide secular textbooks for all children, public and parochial, was upheld. At least a half dozen states have taken advantage of this specific warrant. Much more widespread is the public funding of bus transportation for parochial pupils; almost half the states practice it. However, several states prohibit it, having constitutional restrictions on the use of public funds for sectarian education more stringent than the federal one. For example, the Wisconsin Supreme Court expressly rejected the applicability of the child benefit doctrine and ruled that the practice aids the schools.

The issue of funding parochial school bus transportation resulted in a landmark Supreme Court decision, which has had dramatic repercussions for religion and education and still remains in force today. *Everson v. Board of Education* (1947) was the first major case fully to come to grips with public aid to religious education. It arose out of the practice initiated in 1941 of the school district of Ewing Township, New Jersey, reimbursing parents for busing their children to religious schools. Everson, a taxpayer, sued on the grounds that this constituted the use of public funds for sectarian purposes and violated both the New Jersey and federal constitutions. The state courts rejected the suit, and Everson appealed to the Supreme Court. It split five to four, with the majority opinion written by Associate Justice Hugo Black. Because of the division and the cogency of the dissents, the selection includes major portions of the majority opinion followed by extracts from the two minority opinions so designated. What relationships are specified as being prohibited by the establishment clause? According to Black, what should be the relationship between the state and religious groups? What conclusion does he draw about funding parochial transportation? What are Associate Justice Jackson's principal points of disagreement? What flaws does Associate Justice Rutledge find in the majority's position?

Everson v. Board of Education (1947)

The only contention here is that the State statute and the resolution, in so far as they authorized reimbursement to parents of children attending parochial schools, violate the Federal Constitution in these two respects, which to some extent overlap. *First.* They authorize the State to take by taxation the private property of some and bestow it upon others, to be used for their own private purposes. This, it is alleged, violates the due process clause of the Fourteenth Amendment. *Second.* The statute and the resolution forced inhabitants to pay taxes to help support and maintain schools which are dedicated to, and which regularly teach, the Catholic Faith. This is alleged to be a use of State power to support church schools contrary to the prohibition of the First Amendment which the Fourteenth Amendment made applicable to the states. . . .

It is much too late to argue that legislation intended to facilitate the opportunity of children to get a secular education serves no public purpose. . . . The same thing is no less true of legislation to reimburse needy parents, or all parents, for payment of the fares of their children so that they can ride in public buses to and from schools rather than run the risk of traffic and other hazards incident to walking or "hitchhiking." . . . Nor does it follow that a law has a private rather than a public purpose because it provides that tax-raised funds will be paid to reimburse individuals on account of money spent by them in a way which furthers a public program. . . . Subsidies and loans to individuals such as farmers and home owners, and to privately owned transportation systems, as well as many other kinds of businesses, have been commonplace practice in our state and national history. . . .

The New Jersey statute is challenged as a "law respecting the establishment of religion." The First Amendment, as made applicable to the states by the Fourteenth, . . . commands that a state "shall make no law respecting an establishment of religion, or prohibiting the free exercise thereof." . . . These words of the First Amendment reflected in the minds of early Americans a vivid mental picture of conditions and practices which they fervently wished to stamp out in order to preserve liberty for themselves and for their posterity. Doubtless their goal has not been entirely reached; but so far has the Nation moved toward it that the expression "law respecting the establishment of religion," probably does not so vividly remind present-day Americans of the evils, fears, and political problems that caused that expression to be written into our Bill of Rights. Whether this New Jersey law is one respecting an "establishment of religion" requires an understanding of the meaning of that language, particularly with respect to the imposition of taxes. . . .

The "establishment of religion" clause of the First Amendment means at least this: Neither a state nor the Federal Government can set up a church. Neither can pass laws which aid one religion, aid all religions, or prefer one religion over another. Neither can force nor influence a person to go to or to remain away from church against his will or force him to profess a belief or disbelief in any religion. No person can be punished for entertaining or professing religious beliefs or disbeliefs, for church attendance or non-attendance. No tax in any amount, large or small, can be levied to support any religious activities or institutions, whatever they may be called, or whatever form they may adopt to teach or practice religion. Neither a state nor the Federal Government can, openly or secretly, participate in the affairs of any religious organizations or groups and vice versa. In the words of Jefferson, the clause against establishment of religion by law was intended to erect "a wall of separation between Church and State."

Measured by these standards, we cannot say that the First Amendment prohibits New Jersey from spending tax-raised funds to pay the bus fares of parochial school pupils as a part of a general program under which it pays the fares of pupils attending public and other schools. It is undoubtedly true that children are helped to get to church schools. There is even a possibility that some of the children might not be sent to the church schools if the parents were compelled to pay their children's bus fares out of their own pockets when transportation to a public school would have been paid for by the state. The same possibility exists where the state requires a local transit company to provide reduced fares to school children including those attending parochial schools, or where a municipally owned transportation system undertakes to carry all school children free of charge. Moreover, state-paid policemen, detailed to protect children going to and from church schools from the very real hazards of traffic, would serve much the same purpose and accomplish much the same result as state provisions intended to guarantee free transportation of a kind which the state deems to be best for the school children's welfare. And parents might refuse to risk their children to the serious danger of traffic accidents going to and from parochial schools, the approaches to which were not protected by policemen. Similarly, parents might be reluctant to permit their children to attend schools which the state had cut off from such general government services as ordinary police and fire protection, connections for sewage disposal, public highways and sidewalks. Of course, cutting off church schools from these services, so separate and so indisputably marked off from the religious function, would make it far more difficult for the schools to operate. But such is obviously not the purpose of the First Amendment. That Amendment requires the state to be a neutral in its relations with groups of religious believers and non-believers; it does not require the state to be their adversary. State power is no more to be used so as to handicap religions than it is to favor them.

This Court has said that parents may, in the discharge of their duty under state compulsory education laws, send their children to a religious rather than a public school if the school meets the secular educational requirements which the state has power to impose. It appears that these parochial schools meet New Jersey's requirements. The State contributes no money to the schools. It does not support them. Its legislation, as applied, does no more than provide a general program to help parents get their children, regardless of their religion, safely and expeditiously to and from accredited schools.

The First Amendment has erected a wall between church and state. That wall must be kept high and impregnable. We could not approve the slightest breach. New Jersey has not breached it here.

Affirmed.

Mr. Justice Jackson, dissenting, said in part:

It is of no importance in this situation whether the beneficiary of this expenditure of tax-raised funds is primarily the parochial school and incidentally the pupil, or whether the aid is directly bestowed on the pupil with indirect benefits to the school. The state cannot maintain a Church and it can no more tax its citizens to furnish free carriage to those who attend a Church. The prohibition against establishment of religion cannot be circumvented by a subsidy, bonus or reimbursement of expense to individuals for receiving religious instruction and indoctrination. . . . There is no answer to the proposition, more fully expounded by Mr. Justice Rutledge, that the effect of the religious freedom Amendment to our Constitution was to take every form of propagation of religion out of the realm of things which could directly or indirectly be made public business and thereby be supported in whole or in part at taxpayers' expense. That is a difference which the Constitution sets up between religion and almost every other subject matter of legislation, a difference which goes to the very root of religious freedom and which the Court is overlooking today. This freedom was first in the Bill of Rights because it was first in the forefathers' minds; it was set forth in absolute terms, and its strength is its rigidity. It was intended not only to keep the states' hands out of religion, but to keep religion's hands off the state, and above all, to keep bitter religious controversy out of public life by denying to every denomination any advantage from getting control of public policy or the public purse. Those great ends I cannot but think are immeasurably compromised by today's decision. . . .

But we cannot have it both ways. Religious teaching cannot be a private affair when the state seeks to impose regulations which infringe on it indirectly, and a public affair when it comes to taxing citizens of one faith to aid another, or those of no faith to aid all. If these principles seem harsh in prohibiting aid to Catholic education, it must not be forgotten that it is the same Constitution that alone assures Catholics the right to maintain these schools at all when predominant local sentiment would forbid them. Pierce v. Society of Sisters. Nor should I think that those who have done so well without this aid would want to see this separation between Church and State broken down. If the state may aid these religious schools, it may therefore regulate them. Many groups have sought aid from tax funds only to find that it carried political controls with it. Indeed this Court has declared that "It is hardly lack of due process for the Government to regulate that which it subsidizes." . . .

But in any event, the great purposes of the Constitution do not depend on the approval or convenience of those they restrain. I cannot read the history of the struggle to separate political from ecclesiastical affairs, well summarized in the opinion of Mr. Justice Rutledge in which I generally concur, without a conviction that the Court today is unconsciously giving the clock's hands a backward turn.

Mr. Justice Frankfurter joins in this opinion.

Mr. Justice Rutledge, with whom Mr. Justice Frankfurter, Mr. Justice Jackson, and Mr. Justice Burton agree, dissenting, said in part:

Does New Jersey's action furnish support for religion by use of the taxing power? Certainly it does, if the test remains undiluted as Jefferson and Madison made it, that money taken by taxation from one is not to be used or given to support another's religious training or belief, or indeed one's own. Today as then the furnishing of "contributions of money for the propagation of opinions which he disbelieves" is the forbidden exaction; and the prohibition is absolute for whatever measure brings that consequence and whatever amount may be sought or given to that end.

The funds used here were raised by taxation. The Court does not dispute, nor could it, that their use does in fact give aid and encouragement to religious instruction. It only concludes that this aid is not "support" in law. But Madison and Jefferson were concerned with aid and support in fact, not as a legal conclusion "entangled in precedents." Here parents pay money to send their children to parochial schools and funds raised by taxation are used to reimburse them. This not only helps the children to get to school and the parents to send them. It aids them in a substantial way to get the very thing which they are sent to the particular school to secure, namely, religious training and teaching.

Believers of all faiths, and others who do not express their feeling toward ultimate issues of existence in any creedal form, pay the New Jersey tax. When the money so raised is used to pay for transportation to religious schools, the Catholic taxpayer to the extent of his proportionate share pays for the transportation of Lutheran, Jewish and otherwise religiously affiliated children to receive their non-Catholic religious instruction. Their parents likewise pay proportionately for the transportation of Catholic children to receive Catholic instruction. Each thus contributes to "the propagation of opinions which he disbelieves" in so far as their religions differ, as do others who accept no creed without regard to those differences. Each thus pays taxes also to support the teaching of his own religion, an exaction equally forbidden since it denies "the comfortable liberty" of giving one's contribution to the particular agency of instruction he approves.

New Jersey's action therefore exactly fits the type of exaction and the kind of evil at which Madison and Jefferson struck. Under the test they framed it cannot be said that the cost of transportation is no part of the cost of education or of the religious instruction given. That it is a substantial and a necessary element is shown most plainly by the continuing and increasing demand for the state to assume it. Nor is there pretense that it relates only to the secular instruction given in religious schools or that any attempt is or could be made toward allocating proportional shares as between the secular and the religious instruction. It is precisely because the instruction is religious and relates to a particular faith, whether one or another, that parents send their children to religious schools under the Pierce doctrine. And the very purpose of the state's contribution is to defray the cost of conveying the pupil to the place where he will receive not simply secular, but also and primarily religious, teaching and guidance. . . .

Finally, transportation, where it is needed, is as essential to education as any other element. Its costs is as much a part of the total expense, except at times in amount, as the cost of textbooks, of school lunches, of athletic equipment, of writing and other materials; indeed of all other items composing the total burden. Now as always the core of the educational process is the teacher-pupil relationship. Without this the richest equipment and facilities would go for naught. . . . Without buildings, without equipment, without library, textbooks and other materials, and without transportation to bring teacher and pupil together in such an effective teaching environment, there can be not even the skeleton of what our times require. Hardly can it be maintained that transportation is the least essential of these items, or that it does not in fact aid, encourage, sustain and support, just as they do, the very process which is its purpose to accomplish. No less essential is it, or the payment of its cost, than the very teaching in the classroom or payment of the teacher's sustenance.

*   *   *

Postscript

Although the majority of the Court upheld the expenditure of public funds for indirect or auxiliary aid to religious schools, following the child benefit doctrine, the decision was far from a victory for the advocates of direct aid. Although the majority and minority came to opposite conclusions on the practical application of principle, all the justices categorically upheld the doctrine of separation of church and state, in fact, resurrecting and giving prominence to Jefferson's statement about "a wall of separation." By clearly finding for the first time that the prohibition against establishment of religion was a fundamental liberty applicable to the states by the due process clause of the Fourteenth Amendment, it served notice to the states that their actions had to be in line with the First Amendment. Furthermore, Justice Black's enumeration of the meaning of the establishment clause clearly rejected the view that nondiscriminatory direct aid to all religions was not a violation of it. The direct effect of the Everson case was to reopen and sharpen the emotion-laden controversy over church-state relations. As to the issue in the case itself, any close decision engenders wide speculation, since a shift by one justice would have the opposite result. It should be further noted that in a subsequent case Associate Justice Douglas declared that he had erred in the Everson case in supporting the child benefit principle. Furthermore, several state supreme courts have not followed the Everson position (public support was made discretionary, not required), but have prohibited aid for parochial transportation. Be that as it may, the Everson decision still stands today.

For the next two decades the disputes over federal and state aid to religious schools waxed and waned as new programs were proposed and then adopted or defeated. The child benefit doctrine, without further refinement, was not considered a satisfactory solution by many of those interested in the whole issue of public aid to private education. They considered it just a label. Some agreed that subsidies for such things as school lunches, health examinations, and police and fire protection are permissible, since they are not essential elements of education and have nothing directly to do with religion. However, public expenditures for such things as textbooks, salaries, and even transportation are directly related to education and would, they claimed, be distinct support of parochial schools. A turning point in the controversy came in the 1965 Elementary and Secondary Education Act discussed above. Taking their cue from the federal government, several states that had previously been aiding religious schools expanded their aid and several other states inaugurated such programs. The forms of assistance were many: busing, hot-lunch programs, textbook loans, shared time, grants for construction of college buildings, and even financial support for the teaching of secular subjects. The most recent survey found that three-fourths of the states provided funds for some purpose or other.

This created a flurry of litigation throughout the country; at one point, there were more than a dozen lawsuits on aid to parochial schools. A few upheld on narrow grounds certain forms of aid. One example was *Board of Education v. Allen* (1968) in which the Supreme Court found constitutional the lending by New York of textbooks for secular subjects to sectarian schools in the state. On the same day, however, the Court gave the opponents of federal aid a strong boost. In *Flast v. Cohen,* it reversed a 45-year-old position by holding that a taxpayer had enough interest or standing in court to bring suit on federal grants to religious institutions.

In 1971, the Court further reviewed some of these practices in two companion cases, *Lemon v. Kurtzman* and *Earle v. Dicenso,* and a separate case, *Tilton v. Richardson.* The first arose over a Pennsylvania statute that reimbursed nonpublic schools for the cost of teachers' salaries, textbooks, and instructional materials; the second dealt with the direct payment by Rhode Island of a portion of the salary of nonpublic school teachers. Chief Justice Warren Burger wrote the joint opinion. He found that although total and absolute separation between church and state is not possible—fire and police protection and building safety inspections are necessary contacts—the programs under question involved an "excessive entanglement" between government and religion. Particularly in communities with a large number of parochial pupils, state aid can become a political issue, and "political division along religious lines was one of the principal evils against which the First Amendment was intended to protect." Burger declared the statutes under question to be void, concluding: "The Constitution decrees that religion must be a private matter for the individual, the family, and the institutions of private choice, and that while some involvement and entanglement is inevitable, lines must be drawn."

In the third case, *Tilton v. Richardson,* the Court dealt with the expenditure of federal funds for the construction of campus buildings of church-related colleges. By a five-to-four vote it held that religious indoctrination is not a substantial purpose of colleges and that college students are less susceptible to it; therefore, "there is less likelihood than in primary and secondary schools that religion will permeate the area of secular education." Thus the Higher Education Facilities Act of 1963 which expressly prohibits construction funds for chapels, schools of divinity, and other sectarian purposes is constitutional. However, the specific provision that after 20 years the colleges could convert subsidized buildings to religious purposes is unconstitutional.

In several recent actions the Supreme Court has continued to find unconstitutional every attempt by the states to find means of aiding their parochial schools. Struck down were testing and record keeping funds and maintenance payments to the schools, as well as tuition reimbursements and tax relief for parents. "One may not do by indirection what is forbidden directly."

One other controversial issue of church-state relations which just recently has come to the forefront of public attention is the question of tax exemption for religious organizations. It is estimated that the value of religious property throughout the nation is more than $80 billion. Some people contend that all forms of tax forgiveness are unconstitutional since they are a form of financial benefit granted by the government. Other students of the subject maintain that the First Amendment mandates tax exemption, since to exact a levy would cast a burden on religious organizations. In addition, since exemptions are granted to all nonprofit organizations, how could they be denied to one category—the religious one? Debate over the issue centers around the moral uplift and wide range of free community services and charitable programs provided by religious institutions as arguments in favor; and as arguments against, their exemption deprives hard-pressed governments of much-needed tax revenues and subjects nonchurch members to extra taxes. Furthermore, demand is growing for a refinement of the exemption. It is agreed that churches and other edifices used directly for religious purposes should be free from real estate taxes, but that commercial holdings such as stocks and bonds, apartment houses, office buildings, farms, and businesses should be liable to property and income taxes. In some instances, the latter forms of property are subject to taxation and in others they are not. One recent change is that churches will be subject to a federal unrelated business income tax effective as of 1976.

In 1970, the Supreme Court gave notice that it would not get involved in the political policy question of which properties should be exempt from what taxes, but it did hold that the general practice of exemption was not a violation of the establishment clause. A specific problem related to the general political issue of exemption was the recent warning of the Internal Revenue Service that certain churches might lose their status if they engage too heavily in political activities. Reaction to this was very bitter. Many felt that the government was cracking down because certain denominations were active in civil rights and in opposition to the Vietnam War. Among certain churchmen is a growing assertion that social and political problems are an essential part of their religious mission.

Religion in the Schools

Less complex and drawn out than the controversies concerning public aid to church-related institutions, but certainly more emotional and explosive, have been the conflicts over using public schools for religious purposes. This is true of the comparatively varied programs of sectarian instruction carried on in the schools involving more than two million pupils, but even more so with the very widespread practices of Bible reading and prayer.

Released Time

The first of two major Supreme Court decisions to deal with providing religious instruction in the public schools for those who wished it closely followed the Everson case. The practice of released time developed after World War II as a result of pressure from the clergy of various faiths who were encountering difficulties in attracting youth to religious classes during after-school hours. By agreements with local school boards, children whose parents approved it were released from regular classes for one period each week. They received religious instruction in designated classrooms in the public school from outside instructors, some of whom were ministers.

The McCollum case arose from a released-time program in Champaign, Illinois. Public school students whose parents requested it were released for 30 to 45 minutes from their classes for religious instruction. It was given in regular classrooms by personnel employed by an inter-faith council. Attendance at these classes was reported to the authorities. Those who did not elect this training were sent to other rooms in the building. Mrs. Vashti McCollum, a resident taxpayer and mother of a child in the public schools of Champaign, instituted court action against the board of education to bring a halt to all sectarian instruction in its schools, on the grounds that the practice was a direct violation of the First and Fourteenth Amendments. Defeated in the Illinois courts, she appealed to the Supreme Court.

The majority opinion was supported by eight justices and was written by Associate Justice Hugo Black. How does the program of released time described here compare with any that you know about from your own experience? What features of the program does Black find unconstitutional? What similarities do you find in this opinion and that of the Everson case? What is the decision in the case?

McCollum v. Board of Education (1948)

This case relates to the power of a state to utilize its tax-supported public school system in aid of religious instruction insofar as that power may be restricted by the First and Fourteenth Amendments to the Federal Constitution.

The appellant, Vashti McCollum, began this action for mandamus against the Champaign Board of Education in the Circuit Court of Champaign County, Illinois. Her asserted interest was that of a resident and taxpayer of Champaign and of a parent whose child was then enrolled in the Champaign public schools. Illinois has a compulsory education law which, with exceptions, requires parents to send their children, aged seven to sixteen, to its tax-supported public schools where the children are to remain in attendance during the hours when the schools are regularly in session. Parents who violate this law commit a misdemeanor punishable by fine unless the children attend private or parochial schools which meet educational standards fixed by the State. District boards of education are given general supervisory powers over the use of the public school buildings within the school districts. . . .

Although there are disputes between the parties as to various inferences that may or may not properly be drawn from the evidence concerning the religious program, the following facts are shown by the record without dispute. In 1940 interested members of the Jewish, Roman Catholic, and a few of the Protestant faiths formed a voluntary association called the Champaign Council on Religious Education. They obtained permission from the Board of Education to offer classes in religious instruction to public school pupils in grades four to nine inclusive. Classes were made up of pupils whose parents signed printed cards requesting that their children be permitted to attend; they were held weekly, thirty minutes for the lower grades, forty-five minutes for the higher. The council employed the religious teachers at no expense to the school authorities, but the instructors were subject to the approval and supervision of the superintendent of schools. The classes were taught in three separate religious groups by Protestant teachers, Catholic priests, and a Jewish rabbi, although for the past several years there have apparently been no classes instructed in the Jewish religion. Classes were conducted in the regular classrooms of the school building. Students who did not choose to take the religious instruction were not released from public school duties; they were required to leave their classrooms and go to some other place in the school building for pursuit of their secular studies. On the other hand, students who were released from secular study for the religious instructions were required to be present at the religious classes. Reports of their presence or absence were to be made to their secular teachers.

The foregoing facts, without reference to others that appear in the record, show the use of tax-supported property for religious instruction and the close cooperation between the school authorities and the religious council in promoting religious education. The operation of the State's compulsory education system thus assists and is integrated with the program of religious instruction carried on by separate religious sects. Pupils compelled by law to go to school for secular education are released in part from their legal duty upon the condition that they attend the religious classes. This is beyond all question a utilization of the tax-established and tax-supported public school system to aid religious groups to spread their faith. And it falls squarely under the ban of the First Amendment (made applicable to the States by the Fourteenth) as we interpreted it in Everson v. Board of Education [1947]. . . . The majority in the Everson Case, and the minority as shown by quotations from the dissenting views . . . agreed that the First Amendment's language, properly interpreted, had erected a wall of separation between Church and State. They disagreed as to the facts shown by the record and as to the proper application of the First Amendment's language to those facts.

Recognizing that the Illinois program is barred by the First and Fourteenth Amendments if we adhere to the views expressed both by the majority and the minority in the Everson Case, counsel for the respondents challenge those views as dicta and urge that we reconsider and repudiate them. They argue that historically the First Amendment was intended to forbid only government preference of one religion over another, not an impartial governmental assistance of all religions. In addition they ask that we distinguish or overrule our holding in the Everson Case that the Fourteenth Amendment made the "establishment of religion" clause of the First Amendment applicable as a prohibition against the States. After giving full consideration to the arguments presented we are unable to accept either of these contentions.

To hold that a state cannot consistently with the First and Fourteenth Amendments utilize its public school system to aid any or all religious faiths or sects in the dissemination of their doctrines and ideals does not, as counsel urge, manifest a governmental hostility to religion or religious teachings. A manifestation of such hostility would be at war with our national tradition as embodied in the First Amendment's guaranty of the free exercise of religion. For the First Amendment rests upon the premise that both religion and government can best work to achieve their lofty aims if each is left free from the other within its respective sphere. Or, as we said in the Everson Case, the First Amendment has erected a wall between Church and State which must be kept high and impregnable.

Here not only are the state's tax-supported public school buildings used for the dissemination of religious doctrines. The State also affords sectarian groups an invaluable aid in that it helps to provide pupils for their religious classes through use of the state's compulsory public school machinery. This is not separation of Church and State.

The cause is reversed and remanded to the State Supreme Court for proceedings not inconsistent with this opinion.

*   *   *

Although the decision in this case was clearly and sharply stated and seemed to indicate that the Court was moving toward the position first broached in the Everson case, that the "wall of separation" is an absolute thing, within a few years a reversal, or near reversal, occurred. It was partly the result of a change of personnel on the bench, but three of the original justices modified their position. The result was to cast fresh doubts on the impregnability of the Everson wall.

The Zorach case involved a different variation of released time from the one followed in Illinois. In New York City, the pupils left the school and public property was not used for instruction. The Court divided six to three. The majority opinion was written by Associate Justice William Douglas. It is followed by another strongly worded dissent from Associate Justice Jackson. Why do the appellants believe that the New York program is as unconstitutional as the Illinois one, and why does the Court disagree? In what ways does the opinion move away from an absolutist approach concerning separation? What is the significance of the lengthy paragraph by Douglas beginning, "We are a religious people" and ending, "No more than that is undertaken here"? Why does Jackson disagree with the majority's findings? What does he mean by the statement: "The day that this country ceases to be free for irreligion it will cease to be free for religion"?

Zorach v. Clauson (1952)

New York City has a program which permits its public schools to release students during the school day so that they may leave the school buildings and school grounds and go to religious centers for religious instruction or devotional exercises. A student is released on written request of his parents. Those not released stay in the classrooms. The churches make weekly reports to the schools, sending a list of children who have been released from public school but who have not reported for religious instruction.

This "released time" program involves neither religious instruction in public school classrooms nor the expenditure of public funds. All costs, including the application blanks, are paid by the religious organizations. The case is therefore unlike McCollum v. Board of Education [1948] which involved a "released time" program from Illinois. In that case the classrooms were turned over to religious instructors. We accordingly held that the program violated the First Amendment which (by reason of the Fourteenth Amendment) prohibits the states from establishing religion or prohibiting its free exercise.

Appellants, who are taxpayers and residents of New York City and whose children attend its public schools, challenge the present law, contending it is in essence not different from the one involved in the McCollum Case. Their argument, stated elaborately in various ways, reduces itself to this: the weight and influence of the school is put behind a program for religious instruction; public school teachers police it, keeping tab on students who are released; the classroom activities come to a halt while the students who are released for religious instruction are on leave; the school is a crutch on which the churches are leaning for support in their religious training; without the cooperation of the schools this "released time" program, like the one in the McCollum Case, would be futile and ineffective. The New York Court of Appeals sustained the law against this claim of unconstitutionality. . . . The case is here on appeal. . . .

It takes obtuse reasoning to inject any issue of the "free exercise" of religion into the present case. No one is forced to go to the religious classroom and no religious exercise or instruction is brought to the classrooms of the public schools. A student need not take religious instruction. He is left to his own desires as to the manner or time of his religious devotions, if any.

There is a suggestion that the system involves the use of coercion to get public school students into religious classrooms. There is no evidence in the record before us that supports that conclusion. The present record indeed tells us that the school authorities are neutral in this regard and do no more than release students whose parents so request. If in fact coercion were used, if it were established that any one or more teachers were using their office to persuade or force students to take the religious instruction, a wholly different case would be presented. Hence we put aside that claim of coercion both as respects the "free exercise" of religion and "an establishment of religion" within the meaning of the First Amendment.

Moreover, apart from that claim of coercion, we do not see how New York by this type of "released time" program has made a law respecting an establishment of religion within the meaning of the First Amendment. There is much talk of the separation of Church and State in the history of the Bill of Rights and in the decisions clustering around the First Amendment. There cannot be the slightest doubt that the First Amendment reflects the philosophy that Church and State should be separated. And so far as interference with the "free exercise" of religion and an "establishment" of religion are concerned, the separation must be complete and unequivocal. The First Amendment within the scope of its coverage permits no exception; the prohibition is absolute. The First Amendment, however, does not say that in every and all respects there shall be a separation of Church and State. Rather, it studiously defines the manner, the specific ways, in which there shall be no concert or union or dependency one on the other. That is the common sense of the matter. Otherwise, the state and religion would be aliens to each other—hostile, suspicious, and even unfriendly. Churches could not be required to pay even property taxes. Municipalities would not be permitted to render police or fire protection to religious groups. Policemen who helped parishioners into their places of worship would violate the Constitution. Prayers in our legislative halls; the appeals to the Almighty in the messages of the Chief Executive; the proclamations making Thanksgiving Day a holiday; "so help me God" in our courtroom oaths—these and all other references to the Almighty that run through our laws, our public rituals, our ceremonies would be flouting the First Amendment. A fastidious atheist or agnostic could even object to the supplication with which the Court opens each session: "God save the United States and this Honorable Court."

We would have to press the concept of separation of Church and State to these extremes to condemn the present law on constitutional grounds. The nullification of this law would have wide and profound effects. A Catholic student applies to his teacher for permission to leave the school during hours on a Holy Day of Obligation to attend a mass. A Jewish student asks his teacher for permission to be excused for Yom Kippur. A Protestant wants the afternoon off for a family baptismal ceremony. In each case the teacher requires parental consent in writing. In each case the teacher, in order to make sure the student is not a truant, goes further and requires a report from the priest, the rabbi, or the minister. The teacher in other words cooperates in a religious program to the extent of making it possible for her students to participate in it. Whether she does it occasionally for a few students, regularly for one, or pursuant to a systematized program designed to further the religious needs of all the students does not alter the character of the act.

We are a religious people whose institutions presuppose a Supreme Being. We guarantee the freedom to worship as one chooses. We make room for as wide a variety of beliefs and creeds as the spiritual needs of man deem necessary. We sponsor an attitude on the part of government that shows no partiality to any one group and that lets each flourish according to the zeal of its adherents and the appeal of its dogma. When the state encourages religious instruction or cooperates with religious authorities by adjusting the schedule of public events to sectarian needs, it follows the best of our traditions. For it then respects the religious nature of our people and accommodates the public service to their spiritual needs. To hold that it may not would be to find in the Constitution a requirement that the government show a callous indifference to religious groups. That would be preferring those who believe in no religion over those who do believe. Government may not finance religious groups nor undertake religious instruction nor blend secular and sectarian education nor use secular institutions to force one or some religion on any person. But we find no constitutional requirement which makes it necessary for government to be hostile to religion and to throw its weight against efforts to widen the effective scope of religious influence. The government must be neutral when it comes to competition between sects. It may not thrust any sect on any person. It may not make a religious observance compulsory. It may not coerce anyone to attend church, to observe a religious holiday, or to take religious instruction. But it can close its doors or suspend its operations as to those who want to repair to their religious sanctuary for worship or instruction. No more than that is undertaken here. . . .

In the McCollum case the classrooms were used for religious instruction and the force of the public school was used to promote that instruction. Here, as we have said, the public schools do no more than accommodate their schedules to a program of outside religious instruction. We follow the McCollum case. But we cannot expand it to cover the present released time program unless separation of Church and State means that public institutions can make no adjustments of their schedules to accommodate the religious needs of the people. We cannot read into the Bill of Rights such a philosophy of hostility to religion.

Affirmed.

Mr. Justice Jackson, dissenting, said in part:
This released time program is founded upon a use of the State's power of coercion, which, for me, determines its unconstitutionality. Stripped to its essentials, the plan has two stages, first, that the State compel each student to yield a large part of his time for public secular education and, second, that some of it be "released" to him on condition that he devote it to sectarian religious purposes.

No one suggests that the Constitution would permit the State directly to require this "released" time to be spent "under the control of a duly constituted religious body." This program accomplishes that forbidden result by indirection. If public education were taking so much of the pupils' time as to injure the public or the students' welfare by encroaching upon their religious opportunity, simply shortening everyone's school day would facilitate voluntary and optional attendance at Church classes. But that suggestion is rejected upon the 'ground that if they are made free many students will not go to the Church. Hence, they must be deprived of freedom for this period, with Church attendance put to them as one of the two permissible ways of using it.

The greater effectiveness of this system over voluntary attendance after school hours is due to the truant officer who, if the youngster fails to go to the Church school, dogs him back to the public schoolroom. Here schooling is more or less suspended during the "released time" so the nonreligious attendants will not forge ahead of the churchgoing absentees. But it serves as a temporary jail for a pupil who will not go to Church. It takes more subtlety of mind than I possess to deny that this is governmental constraint in support of religion. It is as unconstitutional, in my view, when exerted by indirection as when exercised forthrightly.

As one whose children, as a matter of free choice, have been sent to privately supported Church schools, I may challenge the Court's suggestion that opposition to this plan can only be antireligious, atheistic, or agnostic. My evangelistic brethren confuse an objection to compulsion with an objection to religion. It is possible to hold a faith with enough confidence to believe that what should be rendered to God does not need to be decided and collected by Caesar.

The day that this country ceases to be free for irreligion it will cease to be free for religion—except for the sect that can win political power. The same epithetical jurisprudence used by the Court today to beat down those who oppose pressuring children into some religion can devise as good epithets tomorrow against those who object to pressuring them into a favored religion. And, after all, if we concede to the State power and wisdom to single out "duly constituted religious" bodies as exclusive alternatives for compulsory secular instruction, it would be logical to also uphold the power and wisdom to choose the true faith among those "duly constituted." We start down a rough road when we begin to mix compulsory public education with compulsory godliness.

A number of Justices just short of a majority of the majority that promulgates today's passionate dialectics joined in answering them in Mc-Collum v. Board of Education. The distinction attempted between that case and this is trivial, almost to the point of cynicism, magnifying its nonessential details and disparaging compulsion which was the underlying reason for invalidity. A reading of the Court's opinion in that case along with its opinion in this case will show such difference of overtones and undertones as to make clear that the McCollum case has passed like a storm in a teacup. The wall which the Court was professing to erect between Church and State has become even more warped and twisted than I expected. Today's judgment will be more interesting to students of psychology and of the judicial processes than to students of constitutional law.

*   *   *

Postscript

Douglas's remarks about religion referred to above and the Zorach decision itself served to encourage those who supported Bible reading or prayers in the public schools and those who advocated federal aid to parochial schools. When examined in conjunction with the Everson and McCollum cases, the resulting picture of the constitutional relation between church and state was cloudy and confused. On the specific issue of religious instruction for public school children, almost all of the states have released-time programs of some sort. In certain communities, especially in the South, classes are held in the public schools, despite the McCollum prohibition. Opposition to the program in any form still persists on the grounds that the state exerts at the very least pressure in support of religion, something it is forbidden to do directly. Opponents also criticize it for its divisiveness and the discontinuation of regular instructional activities during the period set aside for sectarian instruction so that those who have left will not miss the lesson. To overcome these objections an increasing number of school systems have introduced dismissed-time programs. These differ from released time in that one school day is shortened and all the pupils are dismissed, those who wish it going for religious instruction. In one instance, the hour was switched from the end of the day to the beginning because the children were more alert at that time.

*   *   *

Opening Exercises

As mentioned above, no issue involving religious liberty has aroused such an emotional furor as has the question of prayer and Bible reading in the public schools. A survey made in the early 1960s showed that religious exercises in some form or other were authorized in three-fourths of the states and conducted in half of the public school systems of the nation, the preponderance in the Northeast and the South. Specifically, 12 states required some form of Bible reading; 24 states left it optional; 11 states expressly prohibited it; three states had no policy. Up to that point the Supreme Court had never given an opinion on the subject. In 1950, in *Doremus v. Board of Education,* a New Jersey law requiring the daily reading of five verses of the Old Testament and permitting the recitation of the Lord's

Prayer, was appealed to the Supreme Court. The state courts had found the religious exercises in the public schools constitutional on the grounds that they were nonsectarian and there was no compulsion to participate or believe. This decision was sustained when the High Court refused to entertain the appeal.

Despite the position of the courts, there was strong opposition from civil libertarians and certain religious groups. They maintained that any form of religious exercise in the schools violated the establishment clause. Others argued over which version of the Bible should be used. Still others contended that reading from the Bible without commentary (which was forbidden) was educationally invalid, since the meaning would be lost to many children. Even under the best of circumstances a residuum of compulsion existed. A child who did not share the religious views of the majority was forced to remain silent or had to ask to be excused during the exercise, subjecting himself to ostracism, or hypocritically had to join the others and go against his own conscience. None was a fair choice, especially to an immature person.

Engel v. Vitale arose over a recommended nondenominational prayer composed in 1951 by the New York State Board of Regents, the governing body of the state's educational system. The prayer went as follows: "Almighty God, we acknowledge our dependence upon Thee, and we beg Thy blessings upon us, our parents, our teachers and our country." A suit was entered by the parents of a number of pupils in the New Hyde Park school system, which had adopted the prayer, on the grounds that it went against the religious beliefs and practices of themselves and their children and was in violation of the establishment clause. The state courts upheld the use of the prayer, because there was no compulsion for a pupil to participate against his will. When the case was appealed to the Supreme Court, the New York State position was supported by 22 other states that joined in as "friends of the court."

The majority opinion written by Associate Justice Black is followed by a concurring opinion by Associate Justice Douglas and the opinion of Associate Justice Potter Stewart, the sole dissenter. Douglas's opinion is included because he finds broader implications involved and acknowledges his error in the Everson case. What are the issues in the case as Black sees them? Why does he review the struggle for religious liberty in England and America? Why does he find that whether the Regents' prayer is nondenominational and noncompulsory or not makes no difference? How does he respond to the contention that banning the prayer would be a form of hostility to religion? On what grounds does Douglas find the prayer and other governmental rituals unconstitutional? What is the basis of Stewart's dissent from the majority's decision?

Engel v. Vitale (1962)

We think that by using its public school system to encourage recitation of the Regents' prayer, the State of New York has adopted a practice wholly inconsistent with the Establishment Clause. There can, of course, be no doubt that New York's program of daily classroom invocation of God's blessings as prescribed in the Regents' prayer is a religious activity. It is a solemn avowal of divine faith and supplication for the blessings of the Almighty. The nature of such a prayer has always been religious, none of the respondents has denied this and the trial court expressly so found. . . .

The petitioners contend among other things that the state laws requiring or permitting use of the Regents' prayer must be struck down as a violation of the Establishment Clause because that prayer was composed by governmental officials as a part of a governmental program to further religious beliefs. For this reason, petitioners argue, the State's use of the Regents' prayer in its public school system breeches the constitutional wall of separation between Church and State. We agree with that contention since we think that the constitutional prohibition against laws respecting an establishment of religion must at least mean that in this country it is no part of the business of government to compose official prayers for any group of the American people to recite as a part of a religious program carried on by government.

It is a matter of history that this very practice of establishing governmentally composed prayers for religious services was one of the reasons which caused many of our early colonists to leave England and seek religious freedom in America. . . .

It is an unfortunate fact of history that when some of the very groups which had most strenuously opposed the established Church of England found themselves sufficiently in control of colonial governments in this country to write their own prayers into law, they passed laws making their own religion the official religion of their respective colonies. Indeed, as late as the time of the Revolutionary War, there were established churches in at least eight of the thirteen former colonies and established religions in at least four of the other five. . . .

By the time of the adoption of the Constitution, our history shows that there was a widespread awareness among many Americans of the dangers of a union of Church and State. . . . The First Amendment was added to the Constitution to stand as a guarantee that neither the power nor the prestige of the Federal Government would be used to control, support or influence the kinds of prayer the American people can say—that the people's religions must not be subjected to the pressures of government for change each time a new political administration is elected to office. Under that Amendment's prohibition against governmental establishment of religion, as reinforced by the provisions of the Fourteenth Amendment, government in this country, be it state or federal, is without power to prescribe by law any particular form of prayer which is to be used as an official prayer in carrying on any program of governmentally sponsored religious activity.

There can be no doubt that New York's state prayer program officially establishes the religious beliefs embodied in the Regents' prayer. The respondents' argument to the contrary, which is largely based upon the contention that the Regents' prayer is "non-denominational" and the fact that the program, as modified and approved by state courts, does not require all pupils to recite the prayer but permits those who wish to do so to remain silent or be excused from the room, ignores the essential nature of the program's constitutional defects. Neither the fact that the prayer may be denominationally neutral nor the fact that its observance on the part of the students is voluntary can serve to free it from the limitations of the Establishment Clause, as it might from the Free Exercise Clause, of the First Amendment, both of which are operative against the States by virtue of the Fourteenth Amendment. Although these two clauses may in certain instances overlap, they forbid two quite different kinds of governmental encroachment upon religious freedom. The Establishment Clause, unlike the Free Exercise Clause, does not depend upon any showing of direct governmental compulsion and is violated by the enactment of laws which establish an official religion whether those laws operate directly to coerce nonobserving individuals or not. This is not to say, of course, that laws officially prescribing a particular form of religious worship do not involve coercion of such individuals. When the power, prestige and financial support of government is placed behind a particular religious belief, the indirect coercive pressure upon religious minorities to conform to the prevailing officially approved religion is plain. But the purposes underlying the Establishment Clause go much further than that. Its first and most immediate purpose rested on the belief that a union of government and religion tends to destroy government and to degrade religion. The history of governmentally established religion, both in England and in this country, showed that whenever government had allied itself with one particular form of religion, the inevitable result had been that it had incurred the hatred, disrespect and even contempt of those who held contrary beliefs. That same history showed that many people had lost their respect for any religion that had relied upon the support of government to spread its faith. The Establishment Clause thus stands as an expression of principle on the part of the Founders of our Constitution that religion is too personal, too sacred, too holy, to permit its "unhallowed perversion" by a civil magistrate. Another purpose of the Establishment Clause rested upon an awareness of the historical fact that governmentally established religions and religious persecutions go hand in hand. . . . It was in large part to get completely away from this sort of systematic religious persecution that the Founders brought into being our Nation, our Constitution, and our Bill of

Rights with its prohibition against any governmental establishment of religion. The New York laws officially prescribing the Regents' prayer are inconsistent both with the purposes of the Establishment Clause and with the Establishment Clause itself.

It has been argued that to apply the Constitution in such a way as to prohibit state laws respecting an establishment of religious services in public schools is to indicate a hostility toward religion or toward prayer. Nothing, of course, could be more wrong. The history of man is inseparable from the history of religion. And perhaps it is not too much to say that since the beginning of that history many people have devoutly believed that "more things are wrought by prayer than this world dreams of." It was doubtless largely due to men who believed this that there grew up a sentiment that caused men to leave the cross-currents of officially established state religions and religious persecution in Europe and come to this country filled with the hope that they could find a place in which they could pray when they pleased to the God of their faith in the language they chose. And there were men of this same faith in the power of prayer who led the fight for adoption of our Constitution and also for our Bill of Rights with the very guarantees of religious freedom that forbid the sort of governmental activity which New York has attempted here. These men knew that the First Amendment, which tried to put an end to governmental control of religion and of prayer, was not written to destroy either. They knew rather that it was written to quiet well-justified fears which nearly all of them felt arising out of an awareness that governments of the past had shackled men's tongues to make them speak only the religious thoughts that government wanted them to speak and to pray only to the God that government wanted them to pray to. It is neither sacrilegious nor antireligious to say that each separate government in this country should stay out of the business of writing or sanctioning official prayers and leave that purely religious function to the people themselves and to those the people choose to look to for religious guidance.

It is true that New York's establishment of its Regents' prayer as an officially approved religious doctrine of that State does not amount to a total establishment of one particular religious sect to the exclusion of all others —that, indeed, the governmental endorsement of that prayer seems relatively insignificant when compared to the governmental encroachments upon religion which were commonplace 200 years ago. To those who may subscribe to the view that because the Regents' official prayer is so brief and general there can be no danger to religious freedom in its governmental establishment, however, it may be appropriate to say in the words of James Madison, the author of the First Amendment:

"[I]t is proper to take alarm at the first experiment on our liberties. . . . Who does not see that the same authority which can establish Christianity, in exclusion of all other Religions, may establish with the same ease any particular sect of Christians, in exclusion of all other Sects? That the same authority which can force a citizen to contribute three pence only of his property for the support of any one establishment, may force him to conform to any other establishment in all cases whatsoever?"

The judgment of the Court of Appeals of New York is reversed and the cause remanded for further proceedings not inconsistent with this opinion.

Mr. Justice Douglas, concurring, said in part:

. . . The point for decision is whether the Government can constitutionally finance a religious exercise. Our system at the federal and state levels is presently honeycombed with such financing. Nevertheless, I think it is an unconstitutional undertaking whatever form it takes. . . .

The question presented by this case is . . . an extremely narrow one. It is whether New York oversteps the bounds when it finances a religious exercise.

What New York does on the opening of its public schools is what we do when we open court. Our Crier has from the beginning announced the convening of the Court and then added "God save the United States and this Honorable Court." That utterance is a supplication, a prayer in which we, the judges, are free to join, but which we need not recite any more than the students need recite the New York prayer.

What New York does on the opening of its public schools is what each House of Congress does at the opening of each day's business. . . .

In New York the teacher who leads in prayer is on the public payroll; and the time she takes seems minuscule as compared with the salaries appropriated by state legislatures and Congress for chaplains to conduct prayers in the legislative halls. Only a bare fraction of the teacher's time is given to reciting this short 22-word prayer, about the same amount of time that our Crier spends announcing the opening of our sessions and offering a prayer for this Court. Yet for me the principle is the same, no matter how briefly the prayer is said, for in each of the instances given the person praying is a public official on the public payroll, performing a religious exercise in a governmental institution. It is said that the element of coercion is inherent in the giving of this prayer. If that is true here, it is also true of the prayer with which this Court is convened, and of those that open the Congress. Few adults, let alone children, would leave our courtroom or the Senate or the House while those prayers are being given. Every such audience is in a sense a "captive" audience.

At the same time I cannot say that to authorize this prayer is to establish a religion in the strictly historic meaning of those words. A religion is not established in the usual sense merely by letting those who choose to do so say the prayer that the public school teacher leads. Yet once government finances a religious exercise it inserts a divisive influence into our communities. The New York court said that the prayer given does not conform to all of the tenets of the Jewish, Unitarian, and Ethical Culture groups. One of petitioners is an agnostic. . . .

. . . The First Amendment leaves the Government in a position not of hostility to religion but of neutrality. The philosophy is that the atheist or agnostic—the nonbeliever—is entitled to go his own way. The philosophy is that if government interferes in matters spiritual, it will be a divisive force. The First Amendment teaches that a government neutral in the field of religion better serves all religious interests.

My problem today would be uncomplicated but for Everson v. Board of Education [1947], which allowed taxpayers' money to be used to pay "the bus fares of parochial school pupils as a part of a general program under which" the fares of pupils attending public and other schools were also paid. The Everson Case seems in retrospect to be out of line with the First Amendment. Its result is appealing, as it allows aid to be given to needy children. Yet by the same token, public funds could be used to satisfy other needs of children in parochial schools—lunches, books, and tuition being obvious examples. . . .

Mr. Justice Stewart, dissenting, said in part:

With all respect, I think the Court has misapplied a great constitutional principle. I cannot see how an "official religion" is established by letting those who want to say a prayer say it. On the contrary, I think that to deny the wish of these school children to join in reciting this prayer is to deny them the opportunity of sharing in the spiritual heritage of our Nation. . . .

Moreover, I think that the Court's task, in this as in all areas of constitutional adjudication, is not responsibly aided by the uncritical invocation of metaphors like the "wall of separation," a phrase nowhere to be found in the Constitution. What is relevant to the issue here is not the history of an established church in sixteenth century England or in eighteenth century America, but the history of the religious traditions of our people, reflected in countless practices of the institutions and officials of our government. . . . [He then cites instances in which God is mentioned in official ceremonies or speeches.]

I do not believe that this Court, or the Congress, or the President has by the actions and practices I have mentioned established an "official religion" in violation of the Constitution. And I do not believe the State of New York has done so in this case. What each has done has been to recognize and to follow the deeply entrenched and highly cherished spiritual traditions of our Nation—traditions which come down to us from those who almost two hundred years ago avowed their "firm reliance on the Protection of Divine Providence" when they proclaimed the freedom and independence of this brave new world.

I dissent.

*   *   *

Postscript

The decision in this case triggered a storm of controversy that persists to the present. Its intensity came from the combining of a basic social institution, public education, with the emotional issue of church and state. Charges were leveled against the justices of being pro-communistic and atheistic. "Impeach Earl Warren" campaigns were launched. Church leaders and the press railed against the secularization of the country, and politicians were quick to jump on the bandwagon. A movement was started in Congress, supported by the governors of the states, to amend the Constitution to invalidate the decision. Public-opinion surveys revealed an overwhelming support by the American people for religious exercises in the schools. In addition, the controversy was aggravated by the split that developed between the major religions over their condemnation or support of the Court.

As time passed, the emotionalism engendered fortunately began to abate, and most people were grudgingly willing to accept the decision. Several church leaders were now heard supporting it on the grounds that an outward display was no substitute for inner belief and that religion was being restored to where it belonged, the church and the home. They quoted the admonition of Jesus from *Matthew* 6:5: "And when ye pray, ye shall not be as the hypocrites; for they love to stand and pray in the synagogues and in the corners of the streets, that they may be seen of men. Verily I say unto you, They have received their reward. But thou, when thou prayest, enter into thine inner chamber, and having shut thy door, pray to thy Father who is in secret, and thy Father who seeth in secret shall recompense thee." Much credit for the changing attitude came from the calming influence of President John F. Kennedy, who urged the American people to support the decisions of the Supreme Court as the best way of upholding the Constitution and recommended that they pray at home together as families.

Most educators took the position that *Engel* had no effect upon most opening exercises, which were based upon Bible reading and recitation of the Lord's Prayer. It was only state-composed prayers, like the Regents' prayer, that had been banned. However, some students of constitutional law were quite certain that the opinion in the case had been sweeping enough to include all other forms of religious exercises and that the day was not far off when this would occur. They did not have long to wait for "the other shoe to drop."

Exactly one year after the Engel case, the Supreme Court decided together two more cases involving religious exercises in the public schools. *Abington School District v. Schempp,* referred to in the opinion as No. 142, arose from a suit by the Schempp family, initiated in 1958, against the

School District of Abington Township, Pennsylvania. At issue was a state law mandating that at least ten verses from the Bible be read in all the public schools at the opening of each school day. The Schempps twice won their suit in a federal district court, which found the requirement unconstitutional. Following the second decision the township appealed to the Supreme Court. *Murray v. Curlett,* No. 119, was based upon a suit by William Murray and his mother against the Board of School Commissioners of Baltimore, Maryland, for a regulation adopted in 1905 that required the reading of a whole chapter from Scriptures and/or the recitation of the Lord's Prayer. Avowed atheists, the Murrays asserted that this was an encroachment upon their freedom of religion. Their suit was denied in the Maryland courts and they appealed to the Supreme Court.

The majority opinion for the combined cases was written by Associate Justice Tom Clark. How does he distinguish between the free-exercise clause and the establishment clause? Why does he find the practices in both cases to be religious exercises? How does he describe the position of state neutrality in religious matters? What is the decision in both cases?

Abington School District v. Schempp and Murray v. Curlett (1963)

The wholesome "neutrality" of which this Court's cases speak thus stems from a recognition of the teachings of history that powerful sects or groups might bring about a fusion of governmental and religious functions or a concert or dependency of one upon the other to the end that official support of the State or Federal Government would be placed behind the tenets of one or of all orthodoxies. This the Establishment Clause prohibits. And a further reason for neutrality is found in the Free Exercise Clause, which recognizes the value of religious training, teaching and observance and, more particularly, the right of every person to freely choose his own course with reference thereto, free of any compulsion from the state. This the Free Exercise Clause guarantees. Thus, as we have seen, the two clauses may overlap. As we have indicated, the Establishment Clause has been directly considered by this Court eight times in the past score of years and, with only one Justice dissenting on the point, it has consistently held that the clause withdrew all legislative power respecting religious belief or the expression thereof. The test may be stated as follows: what are the purpose and the primary effect of the enactment? If either is the advancement or inhibition of religion then the enactment exceeds the scope of legislative power as circumscribed by the Constitution. That is to say that to withstand the strictures of the Establishment Clause there must be a secular legislative purpose and a primary effect that neither advances nor inhibits religion. . . . The Free Exercise Clause, likewise considered many times here, withdraws from legislative power, state and federal, the exertion of any restraint on the free exercise of religion. Its purpose is to secure religious liberty in the individual by prohibiting any invasions thereof by civil authority. Hence it is necessary in a free exercise case for one to show the coercive effect of the enactment as it operates against him in the practice of his religion. The distinction between the two clauses is apparent—a violation of the Free Exercise Clause is predicated on coercion while the Establishment Clause violation need not be so attended.

Applying the Establishment Clause principles to the cases at bar we find that the States are requiring the selection and reading at the opening of the school day of verses from the Holy Bible and the recitation of the Lord's Prayer by the students in unison. These exercises are prescribed as part of the curricular activities of students who are required by law to attend school. They are held in the school buildings under the supervision and with the participation of teachers employed in those schools. None of these factors, other than compulsory school attendance, was present in the program upheld in Zorach v. Clauson. The trial court in No. 142 has found that such an opening exercise is a religious ceremony and was intended by the State to be so. We agree with the trial court's finding as to the religious character of the exercises. Given that finding, the exercises and the law requiring them are in violation of the Establishment Clause.

There is no such specific finding as to the religious character of the exercises in No. 119, and the State contends (as does the State in No. 142) that the program is an effort to extend its benefits to all public school children without regard to their religious belief. Included within its secular purposes, it says, are the promotion of moral values, the contradiction to the materialistic trends of our times, the perpetuation of our institutions and the teaching of literature. The case came up on demurrer, of course, to a petition which alleged that the uniform practice under the rule had been to read from the King James version of the Bible and that the exercise was sectarian. The short answer, therefore, is that the religious character of the exercise was admitted by the State. But even if its purpose is not strictly religious, it is sought to be accomplished through readings, without comment, from the Bible. Surely the place of the Bible as an instrument of religion cannot be gainsaid, and the State's recognition of the pervading religious character of the ceremony is evident from the rule's specific permission of the alternative use of the Catholic Douay version as well as the recent amendment permitting nonattendance at the exercises. None of these factors is consistent with the contention that the Bible is here used either as an instrument for nonreligious moral inspiration or as a reference for the teaching of secular subjects.

The conclusion follows that in both cases the laws require religious exercises and such exercises are being conducted in direct violation of the rights of the appellees and petitioners. Nor are these required exercises mitigated by the fact that individual students may absent themselves upon parental request, for that fact furnishes no defense to a claim of unconstitutionality under the Establishment Clause. Further, it is no defense to urge that the religious practices here may be relatively minor encroachments on the First Amendment. The breach of neutrality that is today a trickling stream may all too soon became a raging torrent and, in the words of Madison, "it is proper to take alarm at the first experiment on our liberties."

It is insisted that unless these religious exercises are permitted a "religion of secularism" is established in the schools. We agree of course that the State may not establish a "religion of secularism" in the sense of affirmatively opposing or showing hostility to religion, thus "preferring those who believe in no religion over those who do believe." We do not agree, however, that this decision in any sense has that effect. In addition, it might well be said that one's education is not complete without a study of comparative religion or the history of religion and its relationship to the advancement of civilization. It certainly may be said that the Bible is worthy of study for its literary and historic qualities. Nothing we have said here indicates that such study of the Bible or of religion, when presented objectively as part of a secular program of education, may not be effected consistently with the First Amendment. But the exercises here do not fall into those categories. They are religious exercises, required by the States in violation of the command of the First Amendment that the Government maintain strict neutrality, neither aiding nor opposing religion.

Finally, we cannot accept that the concept of neutrality, which does not permit a State to require a religious exercise even with the consent of the majority of those affected, collides with the majority's right to free exercise of religion. While the Free Exercise Clause clearly prohibits the use of state action to deny the rights of free exercise to *anyone* it has never meant that a majority could use the machinery of the State to practice its beliefs. . . .

The place of religion in our society is an exalted one, achieved through a long tradition of reliance on the home, the church and the inviolable citadel of the individual heart and mind. We have come to recognize through bitter experience that it is not within the power of government to invade that citadel, whether its purpose or effect be to aid or oppose, to advance or retard. In the relationship between man and religion, the State is firmly committed to a position of neutrality. Though the application of that rule requires interpretation of a delicate sort, the rule itself is clearly and concisely stated in the words of the First Amendment. Applying that rule to the facts of these cases, we affirm the judgment in No. 142. In No. 119, the judgment is reversed and the cause remanded to the Maryland Court of Appeals for further proceedings consistent with this opinion.

It is so ordered.

*   *   *

Postscript

Associate Justice William Brennan wrote a lengthy concurring opinion. In it he asserted that opening exercises devoid of any religious observances in them, but based upon readings from great Americans or documents of liberty or a moment of silence, could serve the function of developing moral values without violating the establishment clause. He examined one of the problems faced by the various forms of religious exercises as practiced in the country, the question of what version of the Bible to use.

> Any version of the Bible is inherently sectarian. . . . There are persons in every community—often deeply devout—to whom any version of the Judaeo-Christian Bible is offensive. There are others whose reverence for the Holy Scriptures demands private study or reflection, and to whom public reading is sacrilegious. To such persons it is not the fact of using the Bible in the public schools nor the content of any particular version that is offensive, but only the *manner* in which it is used. Many deeply devout persons have always regarded prayer as a necessarily private experience.

He then reacted to the claim that the elements common to the major religions could be satisfied without injury to anyone.

> The development of a "common core" of theology, tolerable to all creeds but preferable to none, is not encouraging, history proves. The notion of a "common core" suggests a watering down of the several faiths to a point where common essentials appear. This might easily lead to a new sect— the public school sect—which would take its place alongside the existing faiths and compete with them. I think the "common core" approach would be sufficiently objectionable to many groups to be foreclosed by the prohibitions of the Free Exercise Clause of the First Amendment.

As in *Engel,* Associate Justice Stewart was the lone dissenter. He refused to go along with the majority finding that the exercises were in any way compulsory or that there were no other viable alternative programs.

> What our Constitution protects is the freedom of each of us to be Jew or Agnostic, Christian or Atheist, Buddhist or Freethinker, to believe or disbelieve, to worship or not to worship, to pray or keep silent, according to his own conscience, uncoerced or unrestrained by government. It is conceivable that school boards might find it impossible to administer a system of religious exercise during school hours, but I think we must not assume that school boards so lack qualities of inventiveness and good will as to make impossible the achievement of that goal.

He found the neutrality of the majority a false one, for it really promoted secularism.

> Permission of such exercises for those who want them is necessary if schools are truly to be neutral in the matter of religion. And, a refusal to permit religious exercises is thus seen, not as the realization of state neutraility, but rather as the establishment of a religion of secularism, or at least, as government support of the beliefs of those who think that religious exercises should be conducted only in private.

The consequence of the decision in these two cases was to invalidate all forms of religious exercises in the public schools of those states that required such observances by law. As might be expected, the same sort of vociferous criticism that occurred a year earlier erupted again. Advocates of constitutional amendment were able to get congressional committee hearings on the so-called "Becker amendment" which would have removed the prohibition on religious exercises in the public schools. Certain organizations and various individuals renewed their attacks on the Court's supposed atheism and intensified their cries to impeach the Chief Justice. A rash of pennants appeared in certain communities on public buildings inscribed with the motto, "One nation, under God." A number of school systems instituted "voluntary prayer" or a "moment of silence" which could be used by students for silent prayer, if they wished. Several of these programs in Pennsylvania, New Jersey, and New York were eventually struck down by state courts. However, a follow-up survey a few years ago, surprisingly revealed that many school districts, especially in the South, continued to allow religious exercises in some form. They persist because no one on the local level is opposed to them, because of the social strictures against objecting to what the vast majority of a community wants, or simply because of the expense of litigation.

Ironically, even though an overwhelming preponderance of the American people are in favor of restoring Bible reading and prayer in the public schools, the efforts in Congress to overturn the Court's decisions by constitutional amendment have failed. This would seem to support the contention that, although the citizenry favor a public display of religion, the concern of most is a surface one and they really prefer a secular society. In support of this, there was no public outcry—in fact, hardly anyone took notice—when in 1968, more than 40 years after the famous Scopes "monkey trial" in Dayton, Tennessee, the Supreme Court found that an Arkansas law which forbade the teaching of the theory of evolution in the public schools violated the establishment clause and was therefore unconstitutional. A further irony is that as government has been obliged to give up the traditional linkages to religion of Bible reading and prayer in the public schools, it has, as described earlier, expanded its role in a number of ways as far as aid to parochial schools. This may not be as paradoxical as it seems, for, as society grows less orthodox and denominationally oriented, support for the educational efforts of particular sects seems less undesirable.

The Tangled Web

As one looks at the present state of religious liberty in this country, the overall picture is one of remarkable accomplishment, but much remains to be resolved. The American people enjoy a higher degree of religious freedom than any other people in the world. Their task for the future is to preserve the delicate balance between the state's role as a preserver of liberty and the separation of church and state. For as American society has grown increasingly secular and more culturally pluralistic, it has grown increasingly more difficult and less desirable for government to be actively involved in religious affairs. However, several questions need to be raised. How absolute should the wall of separation between church and state be? At what point does anti-establishment become opposition? One student of the subject holds, "Freedom of religion and separation are a continuum; if either is pressed too far the other will suffer." Another responds to those who feel that secularism has gone too far in this country and the "neutrality" of government favors freedom *from* religion rather than freedom *for* religion. He points out that this may be the price that must be paid for a system, albeit imperfect, where people of all faiths and beliefs can live side by side together at peace and still maintain their spiritual difference.

Beyond these philosophic questions lie some concrete issues. Although the problem of federal and state aid to parochial education continues to occupy stage center in the broad field of church-state relations, a number of other controversies persist or have recently evolved. One in particular might far outweigh in import the school issue. This is the question of tax exemption of church property. So far there is no indication that the Supreme Court will find the general exemption unconstitutional; as recently as 1970 it upheld it. But as the public finds itself paying higher and higher taxes for more governmental services, it is growing more conscious and agitated about tax loopholes and exemptions. The practice of excluding significant parcels of real estate from the tax rolls and providing municipal services to religious institutions for which there is no reimbursement is becoming a matter of concern. State legislatures and city councils are being subjected to greater pressures, to the point where unlimited exemption from taxation for churches—especially for nonreligious uses—may be ended in the not too distant future.

Another issue involving separation of church and state is the efficacy of Sabbath laws. These laws continue to be attacked on constitutional grounds, but it is doubtful if the Court will reverse itself on this either. However, Sunday "blue laws" affecting recreation and sports increasingly are being modified or discarded by state legislatures, and, although they remain on the books, local ordinances mandating store closings and prohibiting work are not being enforced by the police.

Another source of church-state controversy stems from a variety of social issues which are deemed by some to be religious and by others to be secular. These include such diverse problems as birth control, abortion, euthanasia, censorship of printed materials and motion pictures, and interreligious adoptions, which seem, in the main, to pit Catholics against non-Catholics. The twofold question involved here is whether the rest of society can ignore the religious convictions of one part of society, or whether one part can impose its determination of what is spiritual on the rest. As an illustration, public support—since 1946, federal support—for private hospitals has been practiced for a long time. Most private hospitals function under Catholic auspices. Therapeutic abortions which have long been legal and other abortions now legal in several states are forbidden in these institutions; patients seeking them are not admitted and must go elsewhere. Since these hospitals are partially supported with public funds, can they constitutionally deny equal lawful services to all?

This and other constitutional questions will undoubtedly come before the Supreme Court for adjudication. Minority and special-interest groups have become more conscious of their rights and the general public more inclined to turn to the courts for political solutions. And the door was opened wide for them in the Flast decision of 1968 which recognized the right of taxpayers to challenge the constitutionality of public expenditures for religious purposes. Perhaps the web may be untangled.

Questions

1. What is your attitude toward public religious activities, mottoes, and displays?
2. What proportion of the pupils of your state are enrolled in nonpublic elementary and secondary schools? Of these, what proportions attend Catholic, Protestant, and Jewish parochial schools? Have these figures increased or decreased in the last ten years?
3. To what extent has your state in recent years provided financial support in any form for religious schools?
4. What is the nature, if any, of the released-time program in the public schools of your community?
5. Determine the effect *Engel v. Vitale* and *Abington v. Schempp* had upon the opening exercises that were carried on in your school at the time each case was decided.

Suggested Readings

The constitutional questions involving separation of church and state are analyzed in:

Blanchard, Paul. *God and Man in Washington*. Boston: Beacon Press, 1960.

Drinian, Robert. *Religion, the Courts and Public Policy*. New York: McGraw-Hill Book Co., 1963.

Kauper, Paul. *Religion and the Constitution*. Baton Rouge: Louisiana State University Press, 1964.

Moehlman, Conrad, and Weinel, Heinrich. *The Wall of Separation between Church and State*. Boston: Beacon Press, 1951.

Tussman, Joseph, ed. *The Supreme Court on Church and State*. New York: Oxford University Press, 1962.

The complex issues involved in religion and education are examined in:

Blanchard, Paul. *Religion and the Schools: The Great Controversy*. Boston: Beacon Press, 1963.

Boles, Donald. *The Bible, Religion and the Public Schools*. Ames, Iowa: Iowa State University Press, 1961.

Butts, R. Freeman. *The American Tradition in Religion and Education*. Boston: Beacon Press, 1950.

Callahan, Daniel, ed. *Federal Aid and Catholic Schools*. Baltimore: Halicon Press, 1964.

Dierenfeld, Richard. *Religion in American Public Schools*. Washington: Public Affairs Press, 1962.

Douglas, William O. *The Bible and the Schools*. Boston: Little, Brown & Co., 1966.

Friedlander, Anna. *The Shared Time Strategy*. St. Louis: Concordia Publishing Co., 1966.

Freund, Paul, and Ulich, Robert. *Religion and the Public Schools*. Cambridge: Harvard University Press, 1965.

Nielsen, Niels. *God in Education: A New Opportunity for American Schools*. New York: Sheed & Ward, 1966.

Phenix, Philip. *Education and the Worship of God*. Philadelphia: The Westminister Press, 1966.

Ryan, Mary. *Are Parochial Schools the Answer?* New York: Holt, Rinehart & Winston, 1964.

Ward, Leo. *Federal Aid to Private Schools*. Westminster, Md.: Newman Press, 1964.